European Foundation
for the Improvement of
Living and Working Conditions

Carers Talking:

Interviews with Family Carers of Older, Dependent People in the European Community

EF/93/30/EN

European Foundation
for the Improvement of
Living and Working Conditions

Carers Talking:

Interviews with Family Carers of Older, Dependent People in the European Community

Editors:
Elizabeth Mestheneos

Judith Triantafillou

Loughlinstown House,
Shankill, Co. Dublin, Ireland
Tel: +353 1 282 6888   Fax: +353 1 282 6456

Cataloguing data can be found at the end of this publication

Luxembourg: Office for Official Publications of the European Communities, 1993

ISBN 92-826-6570-4

© European Foundation for the Improvement of Living and Working Conditions, 1993

For rights of translation or reproduction, applications should be made to the Director, European Foundation for the Improvement of Living and Working Conditions, Loughlinstown House, Shankill, Co. Dublin, Ireland.

Printed in Ireland

PREFACE

The implications of an ageing population for both living and working conditions have occupied an important place in the European Foundation's programmes of work over the last decade. In particular, an extensive analysis of the situation of older people in the European Community was published in 1987 as **Meeting the Needs of the Elderly**. This report showed that the population of people over pension age and especially those aged 80 and over, is rising in all EC countries; it drew attention to the needs for care and support for these older elderly. The current studies have specifically looked at the situation of those who provide most of the care to dependent older people - their families, especially spouses and daughters.

The Foundation's studies have sought to document systematically the needs and experiences of these family carers, and to assess the impact of caring on daily life. Research was undertaken in all Member States, with the exception of Luxembourg. These national studies look, in particular, at policy developments and initiatives to assist family carers, with a view to identifying what can be done to improve the quality of life for carers, as well as for their dependent older relatives. However, in many countries of the Community little has been known about the daily experiences, attitudes and problems of the family carers. The work of caring, its satisfactions and attendant problems were uncovered in this research through interviews with carers.

The interviews with carers are the material of this short volume which is designed to illustrate and examine the experience of becoming and being a family carer. The carer's voice is presented directly as it communicates so vividly the nature and costs of caring - and how these change over time. This collection of experiences is intended to complement several related publications* from the Foundation's research on family care of dependent older people. Insofar as these interviews illuminate the daily tasks and difficulties of carers across the Community, the Foundation aims to contribute to the informed debate about improving quality of life for these carers and their dependent relatives.

Clive Purkiss
Director

* 1. Family care of dependent older people in the European Community
     Hannelore Jani-Le Bris

  2. Family care of the older elderly : Casebook of initiatives
     M.A.G.A. Steenvorden, F.G.E.M. van der Pas, N.G.J. de Boer

  3. Eldercare and employment : Workplace policies and initiatives to support workers who are carers
     Marina Hoffmann, George Leeson

CONTENTS

	Page No.
INTRODUCTION	1
Do you remember Marie how wonderful it was?	5
Every week I travelled 800 kilometres between my family, parents and work	8
Even if you're willing to pay a lot of money you still can't get all the qualified help you need	12
I don't know what I'd do without my friend Dora	16
My Mother struggled for so many years and I wouldn't desert her now for anything	19
I feel I'm doing something necessary for someone who needs it	23
My professional life is a support to me	27
Every carer should have a telephone	29
My problem is I can't take the care lightly enough	31
It didn't only mean a lot to them but it also enriched me	37
I want to go back to work	41
I don't look after him for the economic advantage I might get	43
I'm glad we didn't put her into a home: she's blossomed in this flat	46
When my sister came to stay with us we painted our house like we did when our son married	49
I'll always look after her, even if she were to lose her mind	52
I learned to care the hard way	55
I'm happy to have them all here with me, but it's a monotonous life	58
I write articles for the Carers' Association to tell them what the true situation is like	61
It's only when I see the knitting I've done that I know I exist	64

VIII

Caring for my wife is a matter of love	72
I struggle on alone	76
I'm more like his Mum now than his wife	80
I was able to say goodbye to him in our own familiar surroundings	82
I still have enough time for myself	86
Nobody will care for us as we care for the old lady	89
My profession has always been caring	91
Have I let him down, made the wrong decision?	94
Now I'm all on my own like a dry tree in the forest	97
COMMENTARY	103

INTRODUCTION

During the second half of the 20th Century and particularly in the past two decades the population of nearly all countries in Europe has become increasingly "elderly" due mainly to increasing longevity and a decline in the birthrate. This phenomenon of a rise in both relative and absolute numbers of older people in Europe has been studied extensively and there is a vast literature covering most aspects of the subject.

The segment of the elderly population for which most countries report the greatest relative and absolute increase is that of the very old, those aged 75 years and over. Whilst many in this age group continue to maintain a good level of health and remain active, independent members of society, both mental and physical disability are more prevalent in this age group, with increasing numbers of frail older people who are in need of support and care.

How is this care provided? European Community countries have developed services, to a greater or lesser extent, in response to this increasing need for care. Nevertheless the majority of care and support for dependent older people in all countries in the EC continues to be provided by family members who comprise by far the largest proportion of the older person's informal support networks. In contrast to the studies of older people themselves, this army of family carers has been relatively neglected by both researchers and policy makers. For this reason the European Foundation for the Improvement of Living and Working Conditions carried out a study in 1991 which investigated the situation of family carers of dependent older people in 11 member states of the European Community.

One major section of the study involved in-depth interviews with family carers in 9 of the 11 countries. During these interviews, which were recorded, transcribed and analysed, the main family carers of dependent old people were able to express themselves freely, often for the first time. They described their situation, their frustrations and satisfaction, their everyday and longer term problems, their fears for the future, the impact that care has made on their employment; offering a vivid and moving picture of their lives as carers and how they coped with this situation.

It is the voices of these "unsung heroes and heroines" that constitute the focus of this book. Those interviews not undertaken in English have been translated but in both this and the necessary editing, every attempt has been made to preserve and project the situation described in each story. Only identities have been changed to protect confidentiality. Interviews were selected from each of the 9 countries participating in this section of the study; they were not chosen as being the most typical and should not be interpreted as being representative of the country involved. Indeed there is no typical caring situation, each story is unique even if one of the main observations from the study is the large number of similarities in the situation of carers in all countries studied. There are, of course, also many differences associated in part with the amount of support available from formal and organised public and voluntary services.

The interviews are not presented in country groupings but intermingled to give as broad a picture as possible of the situation of some European carers. The older dependent people they care for suffer from a variety of physical and mental conditions, which may generate serious dependency involving the need for 24-hour, heavy, unremitting care and supervision. Those who undertake the tasks of caring include husbands and wives, sisters and brothers and of course the younger generation of carers, daughters and sons and daughters-in-law, sometimes, but not always, backed up by other family members or close friends and neighbours. Some care virtually alone, some have extended networks of support. Some can only be described as heroes, many are on the point of breakdown, nearly all are under great stress. With a few exceptions, most are caring by choice although in many of these cases the choice is partly dependent upon dissatisfaction with the available alternatives or the financial impossibility of considering other forms of support.

How can family carers best be supported in their difficult task? What are their needs and how can these be met by society? These questions will be considered briefly in the final section after the voices of the carers themselves have been heard.

DO YOU REMEMBER MARIE HOW WONDERFUL IT WAS?

Georges, aged 83 and Marie, his wife aged 82, live in a hamlet in Northern Brittany in France. She is confined to a wheelchair, is nearly blind and suffers from serious mental disorders which have made her incontinent and unable to speak intelligibly. But she is "merry in her madness". They used to work as farmers and go on living in their one room farmhouse. The only tokens of comfort in it are a fireplace, cold water tap and a phone: the toilet is outside. One of their three daughters lives next door and although she works far away in town, she is always there for them and a very reassuring presence. Though the future is a cause for concern, everything here seems to be running smoothly within deep-rooted moral traditions and against a background of outspokenness and rough and ready words which, however, cannot hide the affection binding these two elderly people.

"I cook, I feed her, we help her into bed.. what else? She cannot help herself.. we have to help her out of bed as well, and wash her. But it is the nurse that washes her. She helps me to put nappies on my wife, except on the days when she is not coming to help. She doesn't come on Sundays. She's very nice. My wife likes her too. Also there is the home help. She makes the bed, cleans the house and so on. After all there is not much for me to do, now that I come to think of it. There is also my daughter...True enough, I couldn't make it without her. She helps me with the nappies too.. putting the nappies on and washing her are difficult tasks for me. I can't do it alone.

She's been like this for quite a while... a couple of years. She was also in hospital. It wasn't really a hospital, it was some kind of home... hum... I can't remember! They did nothing for her there. Didn't wash her or anything. She was in such a bad state when they brought her back! If they take her in they should do basic things for her, shouldn't they? So I said "Never again! Not this!" I want her home with me. She is helpless, is my old woman now, we have to do everything for her, but we're together. See, now, she's talking to you, but you won't make out what she's saying. She's saying that the weather is nice, that I went out to the garden this morning, but you can't make out what she's saying, can you? We can.

The daughter lives right next door. She comes often, several times a day she does, and at night before going to bed, to make sure everything is alright and do we need anything. She's always there when we need her, she's working though. She also does the shopping, the washing and everything. She's the one that does all that. The other two daughters live out in other villages, further away. They come too.... sometimes they do, sometimes they don't. I mean, it's not like this one here; they are further away, they have their jobs, their children and husbands and all to look after, so they don't have so much time on their hands. The other two really... to tell you the truth, I don't see much of them. Oh, never mind. We see them once a year really. With the daughter living here, it's different: she doesn't only come, she holds my hand too. I don't know where the two of us would be without her... we don't know, do we Marie? My wife is happy 'cause she doesn't know. She's cheerful... she always enjoyed a good laugh. Before you arrived I took the kitten down from the attic for her. We've had it for five days. The nurse gave us it. It's no larger than my hand. I wanted to know what my wife would say. She says it's a dog! Never mind, she just confuses the two. The kitten flings itself onto her neck... it does it to me too. It's very funny. She enjoys watching it a lot as well. It's wonderful our kitten and she loves it. But what worries me is that it eats nowt, always milk and no real food.

I used to ride our motor cycle. I'd go far away, 4 and even 7 miles away,... oh yes, I'd always be up and about, going to town, to the market, the bank, the chemists, the supermarket. I used to take care of everything. But a few months ago - with all those cars about it frightens me -I stopped going on my own. I'm too old now. I fell over once.. I stopped going then, you see. I was pushing the wheelbarrow, it's a very light one, I went for cabbages, we grow them to feed the rabbits. But there were so many of them that this old man fell over! I dropped on the road next to my wheelbarrow and stayed there until our neighbour happened to pass by in his van and picked me up. I was quite shaken by it all... but I wasn't in pain; I don't know what happened exactly and the doctor didn't either at the time. I'd never fallen over before. Maybe I exerted myself too much. At my age... Really I tell you: I'm careful now, I don't use the motorcycle any more. What would become of my old woman if I happened to go? I feel old. Nowadays when I need something, the neighbours take me to get money out and things and my daughter does the shopping for us.

But at night there's only the two of us... If I fell ill too... I often think of this. We do have a phone, but I can't see the numbers any more, they're too small. It's not easy.. oh, I would manage eventually, yes, I think I would manage to dial my daughter's number or the doctor's but.. do you understand what I mean?

So, I'm careful now. I do go out alone anyway, sometimes I go for a walk. She can be left alone. I tie her in her armchair so she won't fall out. For example, I tied her before going out to the garden this morning to plant leeks. Oh, it's not far and I come back now and then to see how she's doing. I go "Yoo-hoo, Marie!" from a distance and she answers me. Hey, Marie, how do we go when I'm out in the garden? We go "Yoo-hoo! Yoo-hoo!" (they burst out laughing together). I look after the rabbits as well. We eat vegetables from our own garden. But my wife eats like a bird.

Marie..., Marie... do you remember, Marie, when I was young and I'd make love to you nicely (and both burst out laughing like two joyful accomplices)."

EVERY WEEK I TRAVELLED 800 KM BETWEEN MY FAMILY, PARENTS AND WORK

Paul (46) is married with two children. He has a full time job as an executive of a department in a Dutch research institute. His parents became ill suddenly: his mother (79) developed Hodgkin's disease and his father (82) had a brain haemorrhage. Together with his five brothers and one sister he arranged for their parents to be discharged from hospital and cared for and nursed at home. Paul became the care coordinator. He made the schedules and the appointments with his brothers and sisters as well as with professional carers and he undertook all the organizational tasks. Fortunately his parents, who lived in a small rural community in the eastern part of the country, had more than an average pension and this enabled them to hire private help.

"It was a hard and difficult task to care for the two of them at home, of course. Neither of them was able to do very much any more and in fact they needed care 24 hours a day. Due to an operation on her spine my mother had sustained a spinal cord lesion and, what's more, she'd had heavy chemotherapy, so she was lying in bed like a sick little bird. The expectation was that she'd die very soon. This was the reason why we, her children, said "We'll take her home so she can at least die in her own surroundings." By amazing good fortune, however, she recovered reasonably well, though she is still in a wheelchair and she can't walk for more than 20 metres. Due to my father's brain haemorrhage he became paralysed on the one side and he also developed dementia-like symptoms. In hospital he stayed in the same room as my mother and they said he could go back home provided there would be someone who could lead him by the hand and care for him, because he was completely confused.

My job gave me quite an advantage - I'm a psycho-gerontologist - so I'm familiar with social work for the elderly and the health service. I knew the regulations and the various possibilities. Moreover I have the gift of the gab and in my professional capacity I have a great skill in arranging matters quickly and efficiently. I'm not very easily put off. For my brothers and sister it went without saying that it was I who was going to take on the task of co-ordination.

After the seven of us had been discussing for a day and a night how we could arrange for both of them to come home, we thought it would be possible to set up a watertight rotation system of carers and that we would set it in action immediately. After all it was expected that my mother would die soon. Though the specialist attending her thought it was irresponsible that we wanted to take my mother home, I went to the social worker in the hospital and told her that the following week I wanted a meeting with the district nursing services, the home help, the GP, the medical staff and all the nurses involved. During this meeting we all took stock: what had to be done and what efforts we could make. The GP would come round a few times a week. As part of intensive home care the district nurse and home help together could take 5 x 8 hours into account. The rest was for us, the children. We made extensive plans and scheduled everyone. On weekdays one of us had to be there each night and day and on the weekends there were two turns, so that there would be someone there all the time from Friday evening till Monday morning. Within one week the schedule was running smoothly and partly because the home help was cooperative enough to work within our schedule. For example if it was necessary she was prepared to come in the evening for one or two hours. Not long afterwards we called in someone through the church who was willing to act as a paid night watch. This took off the pressure for us a bit. Then there was a neighbour who regularly lent a helping hand and especially took care of my father.

We stuck to this rigid schedule for four months. From then on my mother gradually recovered and there were more and more gaps in the schedule.

Now we have come to the point where one of the children is with them only at the weekends. Furthermore there's a home help two mornings a week, private help one morning a week and the physiotherapist visits them at home. But it's a very delicate balance. It doesn't need much for things to go wrong. My father falls regularly and of course there will come the time when he'll fail to get up again. I'm very much aware of this and sometimes I'm very worried about it, especially because I think that if we were required to invest such intensive efforts again, we wouldn't be able to manage any more. After all, we all have our own families and jobs. That's why we've discussed the possibility of a service flat in a nursing home with my parents.

For me these four months were quite a burden. I visited them about three or four times a week and it took me three hours driving each time. Apart from my turns I had to make some extra visits because I had to make appointments with the home help or had to see the specialist because, after all, I had the role of coordinator. At that moment you just do it, you don't give it a second thought, but when things became easier for me I realised how tired I was. During these months I very often went to bed at eight completely exhausted. Looking back I think it was a tough time. Apart from the actual time it took, the responsibility I had was especially hard because I had to decide what to do when there were gaps in the caring schedule. Job-wise it wasn't difficult, though I had a full time job. But I've a job where I can plan things reasonably well myself and where I can easily rearrange things. It wasn't hard, once in a while, to pretend a meeting that didn't really exist, since there's no one who calls me to account. But I do have a rather Calvinistic attitude: work should go on, it shouldn't suffer too much.

I don't know whether the organization I work for has something like care-leave or emergency leave; I don't think so. At least, I didn't use it. Still it would be a good thing if these things were arranged by employers or the government in, for example, collective agreements, so that people could free themselves for the care of others without feeling guilty, because when you work for an employer it's more difficult to manage to be absent regularly. I think that a government that promotes the idea of home care but doesn't provide the money or facilities is a government that's playing fast and loose with someone else's money.

Something I found out by accident was that there is a special tax regulation that allows you to deduct the travelling expenses you incurred whilst caring for someone. And because I drove about 800km a week in those months it was worth the effort. When I heard about this I immediately went to the GP and asked him to sign a note in which he declared that the care provided by us was essential to keep my parents at home. I asked him to do this seven times because then my brothers and sister could take one to the tax inspector too. And indeed, we got these expenses refunded.

Well, why did I do it? I did it out of solidarity with my parents, I've always had a strong bond with both of them. Moreover I wish everyone a dignified end. Instinctively I thought "I'll just do this". What I gained by it is a very good relationship with my sister, whom I didn't know very well before, and a proud and satisfied feeling that we were able to make it all work. When a year ago my mother bought a car, so she can take my father out again, I thought: 'It wasn't for nothing. It's great that we managed together.' Now they have a rather comfortable life together, and this would have been different if there had been no other choice than going to a nursing home."

EVEN IF YOU'RE WILLING TO PAY A LOT OF MONEY
YOU STILL CAN'T GET ALL THE QUALIFIED HELP YOU NEED

Zelda, now aged 70, was a teacher of Religious Studies and lives with her husband, a minister, in their own house in a rural part of Germany. Eight years ago she took in her sister, Vera, 84 years old, who was in need of care. Her four children and Zelda's brother all live far away in other cities.

"I never for a moment thought that my sister would be bedridden for four years. I thought she would live with us and we would run the household together but I didn't think she would need so much care. Even ten years ago she was already somewhat confused mentally but since her husband died eight years ago it's got much worse. She used to be a teacher but she hasn't talked for nearly three years now and she can't communicate at all.

I promised her she would stay with me. My mother died young when I was sixteen and it was she who brought me up. We never really got on that well because the age difference was always too big and we were quite different characters - she was always the quiet and well behaved one. Yet we always used to spend Christmas together every year and she was a very kind aunt to my children. Difficult as it is to care for her, I would miss her a lot if she weren't there any more. I wouldn't say "Thank God" if she died. I don't think "let's hope she doesn't live too much longer" I've adapted too much for that, perhaps more than I should have. My husband and I know what it's like in these old folks' homes; he's a minister. I swore to myself that if it was possible, I wouldn't let anyone go into a home. And somehow I manage, I even manage quite well. It's not the work that's the problem. It's the fact that I'm tied to the house and can't get away even if I want to, the feeling that I can't say to my husband on a nice day, let's just jump into the car and drive to the Baltic, I find that depressing. The day is pre-planned. It also annoys me that I don't get to see my children and grandchildren as often as I would like.

My husband and I have an agreement, that if it gets to the point where he feels he can't go along with it any more I would have to put my sister in a home; but there have been no explosions yet! The members of my family and friends advise me to put her in a home but the discussions never lead anywhere. That's why I never talk about care. It's me that has to deal with it, there's no point in taking it out on others. Sometimes I let off steam to my husband. There's lots of people my age going out and enjoying themselves or going to a health farm but I can't say that they're doing any better than I am.

As far as my daily routine is concerned I feed my sister at 8 o'clock in the morning. I usually give her a softened rusk, because she can't chew any more, she can only swallow. At 9 o'clock the carer arrives. She helps me to wash and change my sister. As my sister is very sensitive to any kind of pressure, due to her being bedridden, we always pay particular attention to her bottom, which we cool with an icepack and then dry with a hair drier. Around half past nine a young male voluntary worker comes to help us lift my sister out of bed and to put her into a wheel chair, so that we can get her to the bathroom. We wash her and then she is put back into bed. At this point the young man and the carer leave, and I am alone with my sister. However they only come during the week. At weekends you can't get anyone. At midday I usually give my sister something to eat and drink, and in between, a snack, usually a yoghourt. Every two hours I move her onto her other side. About 6 o'clock in the evening I begin to wash her, to cool and then dry her bottom and to rub cream into her whole body. Then I give my sister her evening meal and something to drink, everything soft. She is diabetic, so I have to cook especially for her. Afterwards she gets turned again every two hours, until about 10 o'clock when I give her a banana and a cup of tea. Then I put her down for the night. I have to be specially careful that the catheter and her feet are in the right position. I think I'm doing quite well if I can get my sister to open her bowels every five days. I'm happy that such things don't bother me any more. There are also various aids, which, happily we can afford since no medical insurance would be willing to pay for them. I'm through at half past ten. All in all I'm on my feet from morning till night. In the evenings there's only about an hour left when I can relax and enjoy myself. If we actually do leave the house for a while, I'm a nervous wreck. Though she's safe in bed it's still a real strain. But there's no choice, otherwise we wouldn't be able to do anything at all. I put a cassette on for her and hope she won't feel lonely, but I can't be completely sure. She's like a little child. Going to a concert is difficult and watching a TV programme from start to finish is almost impossible.

I haven't been on a holiday for years. I haven't had one free Sunday. There's no-one to take over, not even in the evening for the odd hour. Even if you're willing to pay a lot of money, you still can't get qualified help. I would pay 25DM (13 ECU) for help during the day and in the evenings, but even for that you can get no-one. Our present carer has small children and can only work in the mornings. In the evenings I could maybe get someone or other, but that doesn't really help me. My sister needs such specialised care, because of the ulcer on her leg, that it would have to be always the same person who comes, someone who knows her. Some of the other nurses we've had haven't ever cared for a bed-ridden patient. I had a bad fall last year and had to go to hospital. Luckily the previous, nice carer was still there and she was able to come in mornings, afternoons and evenings. Most of all I worry that I won't be able to manage for some reason. If I could only bring myself to put her into a Red Cross Home for a short time - but she would notice that she wasn't at home. If I could just make clear to her that it was only for one or two weeks I would do it but she'd have the feeling she was being got out of the way and I can't do that.

In spite of everything we still see our friends a lot, they just have to come to us. There's no shortage of people to talk to. My sister used to have a large circle of friends. You can have certain mental and physical illnesses and people stay in touch, but if you go down hill mentally they all withdraw and then you're on your own. Even the flow of letters has got less over time.

As far as caring for the elderly is concerned, I have the feeling I know more about it than my doctor. He doesn't have the day-to-day experience I have. He comes every two weeks to change the catheter and prescribes the things I need. However he's unsure about the illness itself; nobody in my circle knew anything about Alzheimer's disease either. It's an illness which was discovered quite recently, we just used to say a person was senile. Physically my sister is quite healthy and she doesn't know that she has this disease; the brain gradually disintegrates, I sometimes forget things myself. But she seems to be aware of her present condition in some way, that's why I'm careful what I say in her presence.

Basically I'm happy about helping her, but sometimes I get aggressive all the same. The problem is there's never a reaction, or at least not a positive one, it's always negative. When I put her to bed she whines, she doesn't help, she actively hinders. Sometimes I get really angry, you can't be friendly 14 hours a day. If she refuses to open her mouth when I'm trying to give her something to drink, you can't just solve that by being friendly. You can't compare this kind of care with looking after children. Children give you strength, I know that my sister saps my strength."

I DON'T KNOW WHAT I'D DO WITHOUT MY FRIEND DORA

Esther is 72 years old and has been looking after her brother Paddy, who is 74 years old, for the past ten years. However since his release from hospital where he stayed for a year and a half after a stroke, care has become more intensive. Esther lives in a remote rural area of Ireland in a small, well kept house. She looks after her brother with the help of her friend who visits her to enable her to cope physically with lifting him. She is increasingly confined to the house and has few social contacts and no respite from the burden of caring. Her sense of duty is paramount and helping her brother to remain independent is her main focus.

"When Paddy was alright, he was healthy and then just the next day he got the stroke. He became very ill and after a year got another stroke; he spent one and a half years in hospital. They let him out and I did the best I could for him and as time went on I'm still looking after him. He needs quite a lot of day care. He's 74 and I'm 72 and I think I manage very well considering I've only one eye.

Paddy likes to be independent as much as he can and trouble me as little as he can; so for the small things he can do for himself, he will try. In the evening he looks forward to the paper and it's delivered through the window. If Paddy is lucky enough it lands on the table, if not he will try to get it himself off the floor. He doesn't like me to do everything for him. If we belonged to a large family it would be that bit easier, there would be more visitors and he wouldn't be so confused.

Of course he can get on my nerves, he's not an angel. He can get on my nerves sometimes. If he bets on the horses and I have to go down and collect the winnings, he gets very annoyed if it's not right because - he's never wrong, everyone else is wrong.

I have a friend, Dora, she's a life long friend, she helps with Paddy, very, very much. I don't think I'd be able to look after Paddy so well without the help from Dora. To take Paddy from the bedroom to the living room is a real problem. I have dropped him once before and I couldn't do it without Dora, it's too dangerous. Dora manages him very well. I don't know what I'd do without Dora. It's too dangerous. Dora manages him very well, I don't know what I'd do without her and she's in her eighties and is wonderful. The way things are means when you're caring for an invalid, your whole time is devoted, it means you cannot go anywhere. I have often said "Well, I'd like to go to Knock", but I just can't go, because you don't know whether you're going to get Paddy into St. Mary's or not; now I know it does him no harm going to St. Mary's but it's just hospital life again. When I have to go shopping and so on, Dora looks after Paddy, and she'll sit with Paddy, she's part of our life. My place is here with Paddy when I take on the role of carer. I was a great person before I took care of Paddy as I didn't have anyone to care for. For the past 8-10 years I haven't had the freedom - as I can't take Paddy with me when I go out and I can't leave him at home; so as a result I stay at home myself. If you're a carer that's all that matters - looking after someone all the time - you don't have any time to yourself. It's a full time job to look after him, but I can't let him know that as he'll feel he's putting me under an obligation. I don't think it's fair to make any sick person think like that. He never sees himself as a burden. I often think that God is very good to me, he leaves me my health. I have been attending the doctor with blood pressure and the doctor told me as long as I take my tablets I should be all right but the morning I would miss them I would regret it for the rest of my life."

MY MOTHER STRUGGLED FOR SO MANY YEARS AND
I WOULDN'T DESERT HER NOW FOR ANYTHING

Vangelia lives in a small, remote fishing village on one of the larger Greek islands and has been caring for her mother for 31 years. She is now 55 years of age while her mother is 92. Vangelia is married with two children, a girl of 22 and a boy of 17, and they all live in a comfortable fairly modern house built on to the old original family house, where her mother still lives.

The interview took place as her mother was slowly dying.

"I've had her for many years since she had a stroke with hemiplegia 31 years ago. Since then she's been bedridden, well almost so. We used to put her on the chair and she'd sit there. She couldn't walk and I had to help her, but for the past 3 years she's been much more dependent. For the past 10 months she's been totally dependent and can't do anything - I have to feed her. She soils herself and has to wear disposable napkins. In order to bathe her I spread out a plastic sheet, I soap her on one side, turn her over and wash her on the other. It's very heavy work and I've had a rough time.

I don't have any help although my daughter used to help out with her up till 10 months ago while my mother was still in her right mind. She used to stay with her at night - she's done that since she was little. I looked after her in the evening but she slept the night there. She'd give her breakfast before she came downstairs because my mother couldn't get her own breakfast. Then I'd take over. But 10 months ago she got frightened by mother's behaviour. She came downstairs and never went back up again although Granny calls for her.

I've a brother and a sister on the island but they never come, I do it all. My brother lives in another village but my sister lives here with her family but doesn't help. I look after mother. My mother in law is also old but she's on her feet. I keep an eye on her too. As a child I suffered the misfortune of never knowing my father, my mother was left a widow at a young age with three children and I was the youngest. We had some land which she farmed and some goats; she sowed, collected figs and sold them - a rural life. I married last and she stayed with me, you know how it is. I was still at school when mother had a stroke from worrying about how she was going to bring us up. I've never had a break all these years... no and I couldn't let anybody else take her even for a short time, I'm totally tied to her. I can't go anywhere, I must be here. I've never considered putting her in a home because my mother made great sacrifices for me and I must make sacrifices until the end. She struggled for so many years and I wouldn't desert her now for anything.

She knows who I am, her mind is OK - it's just all the rest that's not. She sleeps most of the day. I have to wake her to feed her, She doesn't say much any more. I'll go in and say "Here I am Mum, do you want to eat" - "Yes, alright." She's from Asia Minor and sometimes I'll say to her "Tell me about Smyrna." She remembers and tells me all about it, what she went through when they were expelled. She was an 18 year old girl when she came here and it helps her to remember. She can talk but she can't hear or see. Eh, well she's a very old woman now.

My own health? Well I have nerves and have to take tablets to calm me down and to sleep - I've been taking them for the past two or three years. I don't mind physically caring for my mother, but what really burns me up is seeing her in this state mentally. It devastates me. This winter was very bad. She was raving, shouting, talking rubbish, now she's quiet. She just groans in the night and sighs. She doesn't talk much any more, not over the past month. She just groans and sighs and she can't be left alone now.

In the winter if she wanted something she'd shout "Vangelia come here, I want water; Vangelia, get up I need changing". There were some nights where I had to get up 100 times and I'd get angry. I didn't have a wink of sleep. There's a small divan upstairs where I used to take a blanket to snuggle under; I'd light the stove for a little sit down. I didn't have time to go to bed. Now she doesn't get me up, just once or twice a night; last night she didn't get me up at all.

There's the rural doctor who comes to the village but I don't ask for a visit. I can't get her to Antissa (to the Health Centre) because the woman isn't in a state to be moved. That's absolutely out. She's in a bad way and what could any doctor do? I did get a doctor here to see her who said "What can we do for her? She's an old lady, stop the medicines, don't pester her any more, leave her in the Lord's hands" She used to take a lot of medicines but for the past 3-4 months I only give her paracetamol and aspirin. She doesn't need anything else. Look at it this way, for every day my mother lives she suffers terribly and those medicines had to stop. I've kept her alive through my own efforts until now. I bought her injections and a girl opposite used to do them. We didn't get them through OGA (Agricultural Workers Health Insurance Fund) and they cost anything from 5000 to 7000 drachmas (19-25 ECUs) a box. But I did it just so she could sit up and use the potty because I couldn't manage her otherwise. I needed to be able to get her up so I could put her on the commode. We could get her medicines through OGA but we bought them ourselves so that we didn't have to go there and wait. She gets the 10,000 drachmas (38.5ECUs) agricultural pension, but it isn't enough at all. It isn't only the disposable napkins, three times a day I massage her with white spirit and vaseline which costs 350 drachmas a tin, just so she won't open up (get bed sores). Until now, thank God, she hasn't. She needs a shampoo and a wash everyday. I put napkins on her but she still dirties herself. She needs lots of things and the money just doesn't go anywhere. May she be healthy, she deserves it.

My husband is a good man; he always loved my mother because she wasn't a difficult person. He used to say "Come on up mother" and she'd reply "I can't get up and down these stairs, my child." This house is mine but she always wanted to be separate, she never wanted to be a burden on him. Now that she is old she dirties herself and the place smells however much one tries to avoid it so it's good she's a bit separate up in her room. And she always said to me "May you live long daughter, but when your children marry and you become old, make sure you live separately, neither with your son in law or daughter in law, that way you'll stay on affectionate terms."

What would help me most is if they'd give me an allowance like some others have. She has no disability pension and I get no allowance although I've looked after her all these years. When we enquired about her disability pension I asked the doctor if I could go before the Committee because we couldn't get her all the way to Mytilene. He said "No, she herself has to go before the Committee" And my daughter said "Mum, we aren't going to kill Granny just to get something. We've looked after her for so many years, let's just carry on. She's in no state to travel." Thank God, I've got good kids.

My brother phones every other day and if he comes he offers to stay upstairs with mother and clean her but I won't let him. He's the oldest and remembers father. My sister's never bothered to come although her children visit sometimes. When my niece was here from Saloniki for a few days she came to feed her grandmother everyday; she'd brought her up and found her a husband who's a good lad. Sometimes another granddaughter brings her something to eat if she's made anything special, but it's me that looks after her. I'm her nurse, her servant, I do everything, give her injections, take her blood pressure, everything.

I don't care what other people think, I myself feel a great obligation to my mother and what I'm doing brings me satisfaction. I want to care for her properly, I've never complained and never said a word to anyone nor told my brother and sister "Come on you two, it's not only me that has obligations" I never lowered myself to say that though they should come.

Of course my mother should have remarried, she was only a girl when she was widowed and she had plenty of offers which she should have accepted. She was very beautiful - they used to call her "Chrysa the beauty", but when a mother cares about her children she doesn't remarry, that's for those who don't think about their children.

My main wish now is to marry off my daughter well and for my son to learn a trade. What else? And for my husband to be well. God will give peace to my mother. I've cried bitter tears, day and night, but I'm resigned to it now, and these coming days will bring her peace from her suffering, because she does suffer a lot."

I FEEL I'M DOING SOMETHING NECESSARY FOR SOMEONE WHO NEEDS IT

Maria lives in Ancona, a coastal city of about 100,000 inhabitants in Central-eastern Italy, where most of the population have middle-high incomes and no significant pockets of poverty are recorded. The city, rich in hospital facilities, lacks adequate levels of decentralized and outpatients' structures such as home care services for the elderly. Maria, 60 years-old, has been taking care of her 86-year-old mother for ten years, since her mother was left a widow, and reports her experience as follows:

"I'm sixty years old, and a few years ago I retired from my job as a post-office clerk, after thirty five years of work. I've always lived in this city, where I married my husband about twenty five years ago. He is now sixtytwo, and still works as a skilled labourer at the shipyards. My husband and I live alone, since our daughter is married, and we have a two year old grandson. My decision to retire, some years ago, was influenced by the fact that my daughter had just married and set up house, and had decided to have a baby. I identified myself immediately with the grandmother's role, convinced that every day I would be able to visit my daughter who works, and take care of my grandson, cook for them and so on. I could finally devote myself to rearranging the furnishings of our home, changing the curtains, and maybe even getting up later in the morning, all things which I had neglected when our daughter was still at home and I had to go out to work... All these expectations of mine though had to be revised as soon as I realised, about three years ago, that my 86 year old mother was starting to have some difficulties in moving and doing things. Nothing sudden, but the consequences of her slow and continuous decline began to be quite noticeable to me. As a matter of fact, she still lives alone in her old flat, downtown, about twenty minutes away by car, but she hardly gets out of the house, and in any case only with me at her side. At home, she moves with difficulty, can't take a bath alone, and doesn't have the initiative to cook any longer, when in the past she was a woman with a great passion for cooking. Sometimes she forgets to turn off the gas, and most recently she doesn't even go to answer the phone, and things like that. That's why I now go every day to turn on her kerosene stove in the morning, and shut it off in the evening. In fact, she doesn't suffer from any diseases, everybody tells me that it's a question of age, like many doctors also say, but that doesn't change the reality, that day after day she keeps on losing her ability to move and reason.

So I found myself living a life which was quite different from what I had originally expected at the time of my retirement. At the beginning I used to go almost every day to my daughter's to look after my grandchild; now she has had to organize herself and rely upon a baby-sitter, so that I barely manage to see them once a week.

My day begins early in the morning when my husband goes to work and I go to the market so as to be able to cook for my mother too. When I arrive I usually find her still in bed, because recently her doctor decided to prescribe her some sedatives to give her a better night's sleep, since she hadn't been able to sleep longer than three or four hours a night, and the same in the afternoon. As soon as I arrive, I help her to get out of bed and I give her breakfast. Then I accompany her to the bathroom where, with great difficulty, I help her to wash and afterwards to dress.

I remain with my mother all the morning and after I've finished cleaning up the house I try to keep her active by talking with her about the latest events, telling her what happened the day before, about the family problems, her greatgrandson, and similar things. From her answers I try to gather if she might need something which she doesn't say, but as time goes by I feel sad to see that she seems more and more absent.

I must say that my relationship with my mother has changed quite a bit in the last few years, through this experience of taking care of her after my father died. I live a new and more honest relationship with her, I didn't think she could be the way I'm experiencing her today. She has even talked to me about the affectionate moments my father and she lived through, when I can't remember any tender gesture between my parents in all my sixty years. I see things differently now. At night I often think of my mother, and I wonder if she's asleep, if I had turned off her kerosene heating, or her gas... I had never thought so much about death, before. Nowadays my mother's situation makes me think quite a bit about it. Also I don't have any other old relatives besides my mother; all her sisters have already died and although she has some cousins we never saw each other frequently. So that, if she dies, with her death I will lose the last close relative on my side since I'm an only child, while my husband has still got brothers and sisters... I usually stay at my mother's until after lunch which I help her to eat and then to go to bed. While she sleeps I take the opportunity of coming back home where I stay till my husband comes back from work at about half past five in the afternoon. Shortly afterwards I go back to my mother's, often my husband accompanies me, and I remain with her till supper when I give her her medicines and put her back to bed. Once I've come back home at night I often start thinking about my mother; I'm afraid that she won't be able to sleep or that she might fall out of bed and things like that. I see her in every corner of my house and these kind of thoughts make it difficult for me to fall asleep right away. That's why sometimes, when I see my mother particularly low I prefer to stay and sleep with her. This situation started gradually about three years ago when my mother showed the first signs of difficulty, but if she has deteriorated in such a short time, I wonder what might happen in the near future. We have already thought about the idea of living together with my mother but our flats are both too small and we can't afford a new house. If the situation doesn't change, though, I will have to decide to pay for some home help to take care of her, and that's also very expensive. In fact, she is officially still self-sufficient so she doesn't get any assistance payment, nor would she get any home help from the town council's social services. The only thing I hope is that she won't have to be admitted to a nursing home.

As a matter of fact, I have the feeling that my neighbours as well as other people I know respect me more since they have realized that I take care of my mother in such a way during the day. But for me it's something normal, I feel useful, I feel that I'm doing something for someone who needs it. My husband, too, has been surprised to see how well I have been able to organize myself, he never thought that I could manage it either physically or mentally although, I must say, in the last few months I feel more and more tired. The only person who doesn't like this situation is my daughter who reacted negatively when I started to take care of my mother more intensively, probably because she had to employ a baby-sitter. I'm sorry for that, but I had to choose, and I've chosen to take care of my mother."

MY PROFESSIONAL LIFE IS A SUPPORT TO ME

Conchita is a 61 year old widow living with her 78 year old mother in a residential area of Lisbon. Her mother is very dependent, suffering from cancer and almost total blindness. Conchita works as a teacher in a primary school though she too has cancer. She has three brothers who give her no help whatsoever in caring for their mother so she manages alone.

"When my husband was still alive we lived in another area of Lisbon near the rest of the family. However there were so many problems and family conflicts that eventually we had to move away and came to live here with my mother. Her health problems began about eight years ago. Before that she took care of her garden and was able to do the chores around the house. Now she's completely dependent and can't even express herself. We're all alone here and have no contact with our family; they decided to keep away.

I do get some daily help from the local authority in the form of a home help. Even so my day begins at 5.30 a.m. I get up, cook the meals, take breakfast to my mother, make her bed and then go out to work. When I get back in the afternoon I have to do the shopping, take care of my mother and then prepare our dinner, which we have together. Then we sit and watch TV and I put my mother to bed as late as possible.

My professional life, as a teacher, gives me a lot of psychological support. They like me at the school and think well of me but I can only talk very occasionally and superficially with my colleagues about my home problems. I also get a lot of support from the neighbours, they give me a lot of moral support.

I have conflicts with my mother. Although she always appears to agree with me she'll often burst into tears if I do make certain decisions. It's very difficult to manage in this sort of situation. My nerves have become very frayed but that's what keeps me alive! As old women we very often have our crises of stubbornness.

Financially it isn't easy. Once I organized a family meeting to discuss the economic help I needed but at the end everyone refused to accept any responsibility, so I only have my own salary and my mother's pension.

I've other needs too, just to be able to get out and about a bit or have some company at home. I'd like to be able to go out for a walk or even to go on holiday, but my own health problems also restrict me in that. I'd like to learn something new and to read more but I just don't have time for those sort of things.

I wish I could give my mother everything she needs but I can only give what I'm able. If there was just somebody to be at home to talk to her and to keep her company she'd feel so much better. I would also like to have more help at home. If I had more money I could pay someone to do the housekeeping and then I'd have some free time and might not feel so tired.

I also worry about my own future. Death is always sad but it is inevitable. I don't have much more time myself and I fear becoming dependent. If that were to happen I'd prefer to stay at home and to have someone take care of me but I have no one. Maybe I'd just have to go into an Institution but I'd only do that if I didn't have the strength to do anything else. That's also what would happen to my mother if I became dependent. In that case my brothers would be forced to make the decision.

I feel that after I retire I'd like to give about three hours a day to taking care of old people so that I'd have something to do and at the same time help other people to stay in their own homes. That's usually the best way I think."

EVERY CARER SHOULD HAVE A TELEPHONE

Kate is in her early 50s and has been caring for her mother, aged 83, for the past four years She lives just outside a large town in the southern part of the Republic of Ireland in a comfortable house with her husband and mother.

"I've been caring for my mother for four years without a break. Mother was living alone independently but on the other side of town; then she had a breakdown. Her main problem is deep anxiety and extreme depression. It's hard to cope on my own because no matter what I do I can't get her to relax or enjoy life any more. I can only do my best - but it doesn't seem to make any difference.

After she was released from hospital I had no option but to bring her back here as I had my family and I couldn't let her go home alone. I feel I had no choice but it isn't that I resent doing it. I do resent some things though, like having no help from anyone for such a long time. My mother was very independent, out going and friendly. It's now difficult for her to be so dependent, so dependent on me. It was very strange for me too particularly as, having no children of my own, I wasn't used to being the mother. I had to become the mother to my own mother which is very difficult. In the beginning, when she had her breakdown, I was a bit dismayed with the reaction of relatives really, as it was a nervous breakdown. There was no support, no help and I became even more isolated.

It's very difficult to keep in contact with people, everyone's going their own way. I just lose track of people. I try to pick up the telephone, I have one very good friend and it's great just to pick up the phone if I'm having a bad day. Every carer should have a telephone.

It's hard having her living in the house, especially after being used to space, to coming and going as I pleased, to peace and quiet. I just don't get that any more. It's not only about leaving the house, but even about leaving the room - "Where are you?" "Are you upstairs?" If she's upstairs "Will you come up?", if I'm in the garden there's constant questions, "When are you coming in?", "Coming in now?"

It's 4 years since I've had a holiday. I really don't know how my mother would react to being taken in somewhere for a couple of weeks. I think in my mother's situation it would be better to get someone to our home to stay. If she was physically disabled it would be different. You see, there's a lot of extra work involved. Every old person does not have to same control over their body, so it creates that extra bit of washing and so on. It's not a dreadful problem, but it still creates work.

Every so often I just have to get away - go into town, meet friends, but it's always in the back of my mind what will she do when I'm out. It's very difficult to relax. She's constantly waiting for my return. When I found myself in this situation of having to care for her I also needed to make some kind of money. I decided play groups in the morning would be ideal, so now I run them Monday to Friday here in my house. When she's in a good mood she'll help with the playgroup. While I do find it difficult having to care for her, I don't feel my life is ruined because I lead a very full life and I had many years of freedom to do just what I wanted. I wasn't tied down till recently so I feel no frustration.

I don't think I'm wonderful. In the evening after supper I try to prepare for the playgroup. I find this relaxing. It just helps me unwind. Well I don't want to show that it's a strain, I don't want her to feel bad. I do worry about becoming ill, I just can't afford to be ill. What would happen to my mother, there's no one else to stop in even for a short time?"

MY PROBLEM IS I CAN'T TAKE THE CARE LIGHTLY ENOUGH

Helga gave up her job in education when she took over the care of her 82 year old father-in-law two years ago. Her husband, Dieter, works for a television station as a cameraman and the couple live in their own house in Hamburg in Northern Germany.

"The problem was we had to decide at short notice two years ago whether or not to take my father-in-law into our care. We never used to have much to do with him as he and my husband didn't get on and it wasn't until he became unwell that contact was re-established. He and my husband's mother are divorced and the bad relationship with his first wife was somehow transferred onto his son. It didn't matter what my husband and the grandchildren did, it was always wrong. He regrets that now. His second wife died two years ago and that was a tremendous upheaval. After that he was living on his own in Berlin and a neighbour was looking after him as best she could. If he'd stayed in Berlin he would have had to go into a home but his health was so bad that his doctor suggested that we make his last couple of months as enjoyable as possible. We didn't want to put him into a home, especially not in Berlin and so we decided to bring him here although he was frightened by the move from his flat to a completely new and strange environment. The new surroundings and roads he was unfamiliar with made him go into a severe depression. He's a bit more like his normal self now. Our GP here told us that his heart was so good that he could last for a long, long time yet. Apart from the pulmonary emphysema he's fine, and he takes care of himself too. He's becoming more and more confused but his heart goes marching on. It is, I think, really quite terrible for both parties. There's no way we can live like this for years on end, we're already at the end of our tether.

Initially I said I would take over the care of my father-in-law for two years. From the beginning I set a time limit. In the meantime I found that I overestimated myself quite considerably in terms of dealing with it emotionally. I have no problems with cleaning up after him, thank God, but dealing with his depression is another story. He can be very uncontrolled and ill tempered. Then he moans from morning till night. I'm not able to distance myself from it, I take it all personally which has made me very ill. I now have this serious intestinal illness which is a clear sign of the mental strain.

I washed and dressed him myself until six months ago; it was terrible. I couldn't do anything right and there was another problem. He fell in love with me and wanted to marry me! He was jealous of my husband and would have happily thrown him out of the house and as both of them are hot-headed they came to blows. That was it! I decided I no longer wanted the close physical proximity which washing and dressing entails. For the last year someone from the outpatient care services has been coming in to wash and dress him every day. Also for the last month a young male social worker has also been coming once a week at lunch time for an hour to take him for a walk and heat his lunch for him. This means I can occasionally get away at this time for three or four hours. He's connected to a Red Cross alarm system so that the odd time he is alone he can get help immediately in an emergency.

I would have liked a few more hours of out-patient help so I rang various organizations but they just don't have the staff. This is a big problem for old people who are alone in their flats. It's possible for the staff to give them only the most essential care, they exchange two or three sentences with them and then they're looking at their watch and have to leave to go on to the next patient. I don't necessarily need someone to help every day at a fixed time, however it would be good if I could sometimes get a carer at short notice, especially because of the irregular hours my husband works. Sometimes he doesn't find out till the evening before that he has the next day off; then we would be able to get away for the day.

There should be a holiday service. I find it disgraceful that there is no organization which takes over the care of old people in their own homes when the regular carer goes on holiday. That somebody moves in here for a limited time, a set amount of money is agreed upon - a sort of "homesitter", specifically for old people. I enquired at the Local Authorities, the Grey Panthers and lots of other places but nobody could help. I phoned everywhere I could think of, groups, organizations. There was nothing which didn't cost a fortune, not even medical students. We very nearly weren't able to go on holiday. The Local Authorities recommended old folks' homes, but a room with two or four beds wouldn't be suitable for him, we didn't want that. He's a bit of a loner and needs his own room. We felt let down, abandoned. On the contrary, they said, if you dig something up, do let us know! I think it would be good to have some kind of organization you could turn to, without it competing with the community health care centre. Finally the Local Authorities came up with the idea of short-term care.

He felt quite happy and at home after two days at the short term care place and knew his way about there. He even started drawing again which he never did here. It was great, he found it interesting to watch the old people and although he didn't join in he sat there as if he was in the cinema and took everything in. He told us all about it and enjoyed being with people his own age. He also noticed that some of them were worse off than him. This was a very important lesson to us. We said to ourselves, maybe he'd be better off in an institution like that than here with us, where he's continually confronted with the fact that he's old, weak and no longer able. There's always something happening here, at our place and sometimes that must be unbearable for him. This positive experience has encouraged us to set about finding a place for him in an old folk's home and we've already had an acceptance from a private nursing home in a small town nearby. It's just been built. I heard about it from the geriatric unit of the Local Authorities here. In the home there are single rooms with adjoining bathroom facilities. The rooms can be furnished with people's own furniture. They also offer short-term care. We're going to try it out in March during our holidays. If it goes well, we will probably do it by the end of the year.

It hasn't been an easy decision for us. First we bring him here, then we decide to put him in a home after all. But the experience with the short term care has made us hopeful. I'll visit him two or three times a week, I mean, you soon find out if something is not quite right. We won't be able to tell him till the last minute otherwise he'll get too excited. He's so frightened; above all, he's frightened of doing something wrong.

We're kept well informed by our GP, he's someone we can talk to. He's known us for over 20 years and is now my father-in-law's doctor and sees him here, at home. His own father-in-law is very similar to ours. He can deal with him well and we talk to him a lot. He would also be willing to make the arrangements for moving him into a home.

I've been undergoing therapy since December in the hope that I can learn to deal with the situation better. The therapist has told me that I'm just not up to it. The problem for me is that I simply can't admit that to myself. That makes me aggressive, though I'm not usually an aggressive type. Aggressive too towards him - sometimes I could box his ears.

The therapy encouraged me to look for other solutions but in spite of everything it's still an ambivalent story. It took months till I was able to look around for something for my father-in-law. On the one hand I had a bad conscience, on the other hand I now realised it was slowly destroying me. I hadn't known that before, I thought I could simply learn to deal with it better. I regard him as an educated and cultivated gentleman who should be treated normally and politely but he is also a child who I have to talk to clearly and firmly and I can't deal with that. I mean, I hear how people from the social services handle him - "Now we're going to do this. Then we're going to do that". And he does it. And it works well. And then I say "Would you please...?" and we're back to square one. He knows exactly where my weak points lie and that's where he puts me under immense pressure, for instance so that I don't leave him on his own. Right from the start I didn't deal with it right.

My father-in-law directs his aggression towards me. He can't unleash his aggression upon himself, he has to unload it onto someone else and that someone is usually me. To a great extent I can understand that but sometimes he gets completely out of control, for example he spits his dinner out onto the table. Then there are other days when everything goes wonderfully well; then he's charming and witty. On days like these he's no problem whatsoever. Recently he's started becoming bitter; he senses he can do less and less. He doesn't like the fact that someone washes him. When outsiders are around everything runs more smoothly, his tone is quite different, but with his own family he thinks he can just let himself go completely.

He reacts in various ways to close proximity. To some extent he feels disturbed by us and by the bustle of life going on round him. On the one hand he's pleased when his grandchildren come to visit but on the other hand the visitors are too much for him. All his life he had a sign on his door which read "Please do not disturb" - that says it all really. But if you don't run around after him, that doesn't suit him either. He's always been hot-tempered and he's not easy to get along with. He does make an effort but his personal sphere is not allowed to be disturbed.

I think these two years have had positive aspects for all of us. In Berlin he was still mentally OK and he said, quite clearly, please don't put me in a home. During these last two years we have consciously confronted the problems of ageing and dying and we've had a lot of interesting discussions with my father-in-law. As a result of all this my husband and I have investigated in some depth our own attitudes and expectations concerning old-age.

The feeling of being tied to the house is bad. We can't go to the cinema any more, we can't meet friends. If friends come here, he wants to join in but after a short while he tries to throw them out again and he won't go to his room either. He has taken over our life which makes me say that this cannot go on indefinitely, that we have to look for something now. That's a firm decision. Apart from anything else my father-in-law's depressions depress me too. My problem is I can't take the care lightly enough. I don't think discussion groups for relatives are going to help me in that. Our friends aren't prepared to talk about it and have said we're crazy. The children have had bad experiences with him and are no longer willing to make the effort; they think I'm mad to be caring for him.

I had to give up my job in education because of the caring. I've already cared for my mother-in-law and I nursed my brother for a year when he was seriously ill - he was an alcoholic. My father-in-law is just the next in line. I've had my life really. Till now I haven't given any thought to what will happen next. I've done committee work for a youth club, made video films with young people, things like that and no doubt I'll do something similar again. As I'll also be travelling to the home two or three times a week in the future, that's a day gone each time. I'll have to consider that too when I'm planning what to do."

IT DIDN'T ONLY MEAN A LOT TO THEM BUT IT ALSO ENRICHED ME

One day a week for a year Dorien (34) took care of her 79 year old sick mother until her death a short time before the interview. Since then Dorien has continued to devote one day a week to the care of her father (79) and her brother (42). Her brother needs extra care and attention because he has a mental handicap. Both her father and brother needed some distraction and a helping hand after the death of Dorien's mother's. They live in a ground floor flat in The Hague, about two hours travelling distance from the city where Dorien lives. When Dorien got a job as a research assistant she didn't want to work five days a week but four because she wanted to keep one day a week free for the care of her parents and brother. When her mother died she became the only carer for the household. There are two other brothers (52 and 47) but neither of them took any part in the care of their mother and one of them was on such bad terms with her that he didn't visit her once during her illness. The other son has a demanding job and could hardly ever make time for his mother, just visiting for an occasional coffee.

"My mother had been sickly for a few years, but it wasn't clear what exactly was wrong with her. When the fatal diagnosis was made we knew she'd die of a bone marrow disease, but we didn't know when. For me this was a sort of turning point. From then on I had this strong feeling 'I should be with them'. I was already visiting them more often but from that moment on I went there one fixed day every week. Because I was still studying then this was easy to arrange. The things I did on this Wednesday varied: I took care of quite a lot of organizational stuff, I always did the shopping for the whole week, I did the laundry, changed the beds and did the cooking, but I also provided them with some distraction because my parents' world became smaller and smaller. They belong to a generation that doesn't find it easy to ask for help and is afraid to trouble others. For instance, their GP, who had established himself in their neighbourhood only recently and who didn't know them very well, hardly visited them that year. And besides, my parents are people who want to keep their pride and independence and who value their privacy very much.

I don't blame my brothers for not taking part in the care of my mother. Though there were the four of us at home I very often felt as if I was an only child because there was a great age difference between me and my brothers. There are no strong ties between us. Furthermore I'm the only daughter, and this probably played a part too in me becoming the carer. What I did miss though was not being able to share responsibility with my family. What bothered me in particular was the fight between my oldest brother and my mother because I could see she suffered from it and it was only after her death that he came back to the family. I would never have forgiven myself if I'd not done it. I'm also glad that I did it because it didn't only mean a lot to them but it also enriched me. Now I know what I'm worth in difficult situations and this made me feel stronger. It's satisfying that I've been able to make their life more comfortable during that difficult period. It also strengthened the bond between my parents and me.

I still don't get much support from my older brothers. When my mother was ill there were two neighbours who had the key of the house and who kept on eye on things. Sometimes one of them would bring my parents a meal. Apart from that they had home care for three hours a week. This was because of my mother's illness. When she died the home care people wanted to stop this help because my father isn't really ill and therefore not entitled to it. I think this is really ridiculous because my father and brother can hardly manage even when they do get this home care. I had to move heaven and earth to let them keep these three hours of home care. I also had to talk my father into not adopting too cooperative an attitude during the new intake by the home care service because if he wanted to do too much of the housework himself, he and my brother wouldn't be entitled to home care. I think it's really outrageous that they make conditions like this, especially because my father pays the maximum personal contribution of Dfl 40,00 (20 ECU) per morning. If people need this kind of help - and for them it's really necessary, after all my younger brother is an extra concern for my father - then it should just be there. It's the least you can expect.

In practice a four day job was easy to combine with the care for my mother. On the day I didn't go to work I could go to the Hague. When I got this job it was an open-and-shut case that I wanted to work only four days, otherwise I wouldn't have been able to continue my visits to them. Nor do I want to give them up now because my father and brother need my support and care very much, though they do seem to cope together wonderfully well. At my work they weren't worried about it very much because I restricted the care to my days off most of the time but I myself didn't think I was functioning at my optimum. Every night when I came home from work I felt dead beat. Very often I went to bed at half past nine or ten o'clock. This wasn't like me at all because basically I'm a night person and have always had an unlimited amount of energy. Now this has completely gone. During the course of the year I gave up all the other activities I used to do in the evenings, such as literature classes and swimming and I still haven't got the energy to take them up again. This makes me realise that the unpredictable course of my mother's illness and the fact that she was going to die had been hanging over me like the sword of Damocles and that the responsibility I felt and still feel is a great weight. The travelling between The Hague and where I live is hard too: it takes two hours there and back each time. At a certain point I asked for an interview with my co-ordinator at work because I had the feeling that I wasn't really functioning very well in my job. She hadn't noticed anything at all however, so maybe this was something more in my own mind. Maybe it was also the result of feeling physically exhausted.

I must say my colleagues and friends were very understanding and thanks to this I have been able to provide this care. When I needed an extra afternoon off to go to the hospital with my mother or father, this was always possible. I also received a lot of support from my partner. As we live together it is, of course, important that he can understand my choice. After all, he is the one who is troubled most by my being away more often and not being capable of doing much in the evening. We would really love to have children but combining the care for my parents and my brother with a child seems quite a task to me. Furthermore my choice to work only four days was also possible because my partner's income is such that I can manage financially not to work full time. If people have to work full time at a minimum wage, it's impossible. So I think care-leave regulations should exist. I don't know whether the organization I work for has such a leave regulation - nobody has told me anything so far.

I often wonder what will happen if my father becomes ill and what will happen to my youngest brother if something happens to my father. I've had a talk with my father and a social worker about a place in a family home for mentally disabled people for my brother. He's on a waiting list now but it isn't clear when he will be able to go there permanently. However I did arrange for him to go there for a week to try it out. Still, I hope that for the time being they will be able to live together in their house because they're very fond of one another and a great support to each other. Recently I've taught my brother how to use the telephone so that if something happens to my father he will at least be able to phone me. It's quite a reassurance that he is able to do that now."

I WANT TO GO BACK TO WORK

Antonietta is 48 years old, married with two children. She lives in a village which is now within the greater urban area of Coimbra in the centre of Portugal. Though the village still retains some traditional rural characteristics many of the residents, particularly women, work in the city's textile industry while many of the men work for the Portuguese Railway company. Antonietta worked in a textile factory until her mother-in-law (86 years old) started having health problems caused by recurrent pulmonary disease, and became dependent.

Her mother-in-law lives in the same village about a 30 minute walk from Antonietta's home.

"My mother-in-law was always a very active person. Even when she was bent double she still went to the farm and did some work there. When she became ill I used to go several times a day to take care of her. Every time I arrived there I was worried I'd find her dead. Everything was dirty and I had a real job to get the place cleaned up again. I've already looked after my own parents when they were ill and if I hadn't taken care of my mother-in-law everybody in the village would think that my husband and I were behaving very badly.

About a year ago, on New Year's Day, my husband was out at work on the railways. My daughter and I had to stay with mother-in-law until 4.00 in the morning and then walk home and when the situation became worse I had to stay overnight. We couldn't go on like that so we brought the old lady here to our house although it meant that I had to leave my work so that I could look after her.

We provided a small bedroom for her in our house. She improved a lot and now she can get up, go to the bathroom and eat by herself, which is a very good thing. Sometimes it's a bit difficult to take care of her because she's very obstinate; she wants to do only what she wants.

I have to look after my mother-in-law because she has no other children. At the weekend my husband drives her to her own home and when he's on the weekend shift he drives her there during the week because if he doesn't take her home regularly she goes on and on about it.

I have problems with my back and all this extra work is bad for me, but I know that people in the village say I'm a good daughter-in-law, even better than my husband. He isn't so patient. When friends come to pay a visit my mother-in-law tells them that I am better than her son, but actually the two of them are very close. My husband lost his father when he was very young.

Even if I got someone else to care for her I'm sure she wouldn't accept it. If she could only go back to her own home I would go and give her all the necessary help and then I'd have a more independent life. I could then go back to work, but I'm afraid she'll get worse again during the winter.

Of course now that I've lost my salary we are hard up but my mother-in-law doesn't seem to understand this. She thinks we should take care of her because she gives us all her pension money but it isn't nearly enough to cover all the expenses. I think it would be a good thing if we received some payment in order to help in such a situation.

I still think about going back to work but my mother-in-law doesn't want me to go out. When she was very ill she didn't even want her son to go to work. She threatened to die one day so that when he got back he wouldn't find her alive. It was a very difficult period.

I can see that I am setting an example to my own children, but you never know what the future will hold. They might leave the village and find employment far away. Sometimes my daughter asks me if she will have to face the same difficulties in her life, so many sacrifices.... How can I answer that?"

I DON'T LOOK AFTER HIM FOR THE ECONOMIC ADVANTAGE I MIGHT GET

Teresa, who is 70, lives in a small town of about two thousand inhabitants, near the Adriatic coast in Central Italy. Recent industrialization of the area has not yet eliminated signs of its farming history, as can clearly be seen from the structure of the houses, which are mostly one family with a surrounding plot of land where the older people cultivate their kitchen gardens. Most of the elderly, both male and female, who live in this area get a farmer's pension. This, together with their kitchen garden, allows them to face old age with fewer economic difficulties than those living in generally more expensive urban areas. Teresa talks about her experience in looking after Vittorio, who is presently in a nursing home.

"Now that I'm seventy I can say that my life has changed a lot from when, thirty years ago, I met the person I'm looking after now. At that time Vittorio still lived with his parents in a mansion in the same town as myself. His family was rich and owned the land which for generations my family had worked on. I also worked on that land when I was young, first with my father and then, seeing my father never gave me any money, I went elsewhere as a farm labourer, always on Vittorio's property.

I worked in the fields for twenty years until it began to get too tiring for me and I changed jobs, ending up as a maid in Vittorio's family house. This happened thirty years ago. Over the years, though I continued to wash the floors and cook, I became a person of confidence to him and Vittorio, who's an only child, asked me to continue to clean the house and cook for him when his parents died. I'd usually go to work in Vittorio's house in the morning and come back in the evening. We'd eat lunch together, then in the evening I'd prepare his meal and go back home, in the country a few miles out of town, where I lived with my brothers, sisters and their children. I never thought, at that time, that Vittorio would ask me to marry him and that today I'd be living the way I am. For a long time we'd been on first name terms and there had been a bit of romance between us in the past, but that was long ago. So, when he asked me to marry him, about fifteen years ago, I told him I wouldn't because everybody in town would think I was doing it for the money. He then asked me to move into his house, which I did a short while afterwards. When later he started talking about marriage again I told him that at that point it wasn't necessary any more, because we were already living like a married couple.

I know of other women from my area who went to live with their employers, I'm certainly not the only one, but for a long time the people in town talked of nothing else. I, an unmarried woman, going to live with the richest man in town who was also sixteen years older than me; you just can't imagine the reaction! It wasn't easy, the relationship with my family deteriorated as they never approved of my decision. My sisters said I was crazy, that I should be ashamed, but I had known him for such a long time, going to his house every morning and leaving in the evening, that moving in was certainly no problem for me. On the contrary, I could finally do up the house as I wanted to. And among the best moments during those years, I shall never forget the first time we went away together, Vittorio and I, on holiday, ten years ago. It was the first time I had ever been to a hotel in my life, the first time I had to show my identity card...

When I went to live with him, fifteen years ago, everybody started calling me the "lady of the house", and said that it was I who was the boss, but I never took any notice. And even if I collect his pension by proxy, enough to pay the nursing home, and he has made his will, I still have my small farm labourer's pension (about 500,000 lire a month or 264 ECU). Of course, if I only had that to live on, I wouldn't be able to live the way I do.

You can now understand why I'm still grateful and attached to him after all these years. Even today, even after Vittorio had a stroke, four years ago, which paralysed his right side and left him unable to walk, dress himself and eat properly, making him incontinent and able to talk only with great difficulty. At first I tried to look after him on my own, but after a short time I thought he was going to die and not knowing what to do, I put him in hospital. There the doctors told me to put him into a nursing home. I tried to take him back home and get domestic help so that I had more time to look after him, but I still couldn't take care of him as I wanted to, so after having talked it over with Vittorio, I decided to take him to the nursing home.

For two years now, since he was taken in, I go to the nursing home every morning around seven o'clock and bring him his clean laundry, I help the nurses get him out of bed and together we wash and dress him. Then he has breakfast, I put him in a wheelchair, and I tell him about how I spent the previous evening. Then I put him near a window so he can look outside, see the people in the street and nearly see his own house, which is only seventy or eighty metres away.

About eleven I go back home, collect the meal which in the meantime has been prepared by the home help, who comes every day to clean the house, and take it to Vittorio. I feed him, put him back to bed and go home again. In the afternoon I go back to see Vittorio, give him coffee with biscuits, stay a couple of hours and then go back home.

I have to say that the nursing home staff treat Vittorio very well, perhaps because he's one of the few people who pays his monthly charge [that is, without the town council paying a part, which it usually does in the case of disabled elderly people]: Vittorio is always clean and well looked after, someone always comes when he calls and the doctor also visits him when required. I couldn't cope with him at home, I couldn't move him or change him and it's really as if he had chosen to go to the nursing home, so I wouldn't have to worry about him."

I'M GLAD WE DIDN'T PUT HER INTO A HOME: SHE'S BLOSSOMED IN THIS FLAT

Else and Jette are two sisters who together look after their 86 year old mother. All three of them live in Copenhagen. Else is aged 56, is divorced and now lives alone in her flat, whilst Jette is aged 43 and lives with her husband and 13 year old son in their own house in one of Copenhagen's suburbs.

"We've been looking after Mum now for 11 years" explains Else. "For the first five years, she was well enough to live in her own flat after Dad died, but for the last 6 years she has been living in this service flat provided by the council."

"In a way, it's a lot better here" says Jette. "We have less worry, because there is professional help available, but Mum still needs us and the help we can give. It's a comfort her being here, now that she suffers so much from dementia, which started about three years ago."

"Before that Mum had just been old, I suppose, " says Else "and just needed someone to look after her and help with the daily chores. Now that she's moved to this service flat though, I think she definitely improved. Wouldn't you say so, Jette?"

"Certainly. I even feel that her dementia has improved, or maybe it's just a combination of so many things. At least, what we do now is not as cumbersome and demanding, and the professional supervision is a comfort. Like knowing that nothing drastic can happen. It was heavy going while Mum still lived at home. Visits every day, shopping and cooking. Luckily, I suppose, Mum could dress and wash herself, and there was a home help from the council who did the cleaning. No, we've not really felt that the authorities weren't doing their bit. And today, we visit Mum a couple of times a week to do the shopping and laundering."

"Even so," adds Else "I give Mum a call every day. Comfort like, for both of us really. And whenever she feels up to it, and we can cope, we take her out or bring her home for a visit. She likes that."

"I'm lucky too," says Jette "because my husband understands the situation. He's never grumbled about me helping Mum and not spending the time I spend with her with him. It's difficult though, always wanting to do the right thing. I remember when Mum's dementia was bad, we both wanted her moved into a nursing home. We were sure that was best for her, but then Jorgen at the local old people's centre who knew Mum advised against it.

And now, well, I'm glad we didn't put her into a home, she's blossomed in this flat.

"Sometimes, of course, it all seems never ending. I'm not sure I can keep it up like this until... well, until Mum dies I suppose. But then it's a case of doing one's duty, isn't it? I don't regret it and wouldn't want it any other way. I mean, she's our Mum. It's our way of saying thanks for all she's ever done for us when she could, when she was younger and healthier. I don't think anyone would turn their back on their Mum and Dad. I mean, you don't, do you? And we don't expect any financial reward or whatever from the authorities. No, it's reward enough the way it is."

Both daughters agreed that the public authorities had done a great deal to help, and they were very relieved now that their mother had been moved into the service flat.

"Mind you, we could use more information. It was particularly bad before Mum moved. I mean, we knew nothing about dementia, and we had no idea what help could be got. As long as Mum's in her own flat, she has more or less what she needs - aids and the like - but it would be nice to have more help from the authorities when she visits us. Simple things, you know - a light wheelchair, and especially a commode. Mum's not good on the toilet, and we don't have the facilities at home.

We've tried to get the staff at the centre where Mum's flat is to start a family group that could support relatives with the same problems as we have. But they haven't really the time. Yes, I suppose we could try ourselves, but really we just don't know where to start. Sometimes little problems become hopeless, and you just resign yourself to it in a way. I remember thinking at one stage when Mum was still at home that it just kept getting worse. I mean, when we started, we had no idea what it would turn into, how much work there would be, or what kind of work and you are so very much alone with it. We didn't even know if what we were doing was right."

"The worst though is being away", admits Jette. "Going on holiday is like having a really bad conscience. It would be nice with a family support group so that you knew someone was doing what we would normally do. Of course, I suppose if we suddenly weren't able to cope, then the professionals would take over. But then again, there's so much talk of cutbacks, that you can't really be sure any more."

"It's been a great comfort to both of us," says Else "that we have had one another to talk to about it all. I don't know how I would have coped emotionally if I had not had Jette, especially after my divorce. As for the future, we'll carry on doing what we're doing for as long as it's necessary, no doubt about that at all. If Mum does get worse again – her dementia – I just hope that there will be a nursing home place available for her. You never know."

WHEN MY SISTER CAME TO STAY WITH US
WE PAINTED OUR HOUSE LIKE WE DID WHEN OUR SON MARRIED

It is not easy, in this case, to distinguish the carer from the person being cared for as we are faced with three elderly people, all of whom need looking after, though in different ways. Ersilia, 80, is the healthiest of the three and for this reason the one who was talked to as the main carer. Her husband Rodolfo, who is 84, can still take care of himself although he is becoming disabled. Ersilia's sister, Teresa, aged 82, is the person who most needs help and is looked after by the other two with whom she has been living in their house in Southern Italy for about three years. Ersilia talks about her experience as follows:

"My sister, who is unmarried and without children, lived in a town nearby, but her heart circulation problems were becoming worse and she couldn't move well so it wasn't possible for her to continue living on her own. She was hospitalized for a while and then was supposed to go to an old people's home. My husband and I discussed how to look after my sister. We asked a lot of people how their relatives were cared for in the institution, and we even thought about all going there, me, my sister and my husband. But then we decided not to as quite a few people weren't happy there, the food wasn't good, they were forced to share a room with others they didn't want to and they hadn't lasted long. Of course, we didn't want to be a burden on our children. Apart from the fact that the younger generation has different needs, we also had to take into account the fact that they live about an hour's drive away. If they had lived nearer, things would have been easier. Instead, apart from their usual weekend visit, we couldn't expect much else from them. After all, they also have their own families to look after.

So eventually, after having thought about the long winters during the war where all the neighbours helped each other, we decided that perhaps the best solution was to have my sister stay with us. I always got on well with my sister when we were young and so we were really happy about this decision, as if we were starting a new life. My husband and I painted the house, as we had done twenty years ago when our son got married, and then my sister moved in.

It's one thing seeing someone every now and then for a short while, and it's another to live constantly together day after day. Now we have the time, we often talk about the past, about our parents and other relatives, even though most of them are dead, of how we lived before, when we were young... In this way we managed to bring back to life a relationship which had grown weaker over the last forty years, though never broken, and we rediscovered many things which we had done together when we were young. Since she came here, my sister has taught me to knit so that I continue her hobby which she can't do any more. Even my husband was happy when my sister came, it made him feel necessary again like when we had to look after our children. Imagine, he even decided to enlarge the kitchen garden so as to have more vegetables for the three of us!

From this point of view we're happy about our decision. And we're certainly not the only ones who live like this, there are many elderly brothers and sisters who live together in this area. But the state of health of my sister and also of my husband and myself makes us worry about the future. My sister can hardly do anything by herself any more. I do all the cooking, I help her get washed and dressed. My husband is still able to go out and do the shopping and dig up a few vegetables, but even he is beginning to find it difficult to do many things. And thinking about our age, I must say that I'm very worried about our future because the problems we have with my sister have become ours as well. At present, however, we don't have any great economic problems: we don't have to pay for any assistance, and when my sister goes to hospital for her check-ups (about ten kilometres away) the town council partly pays for the taxi expenses. We only have the "minimum" pension [450,000 lire per head, 235 ECU], and if we had to pay for help for my sister, we certainly wouldn't be able to afford it. Night assistance costs about 70,000 - 80,000 lire (42 ECU) an hour, which is much beyond our means. We talk about this from time to time, and try to keep going. We also have to thank our neighbours who, when they have time, accompany my sister for her medical check-ups. And if we find that we can't cope, then I hope we'll find an assistant who'll come to the house, rather than end up in an institution. I hope we'll never have to end our days there."

I'LL ALWAYS LOOK AFTER HER EVEN IF SHE WERE TO LOSE HER MIND

Henri is 36 and the only one of four brothers and sisters still unmarried and living at home with his mother. All live in Hillion, a village near Saint-Brieuc in Brittany. He helped care for his father until he died and has been tending his mother for 4 years. She is confined to an arm chair.

The house is small and ill-equipped; the mother has her own little room; the son sleeps in the kitchen which is also the main room. His brother lives on the first floor with his wife and children.

Unemployment suited Henri and although he had just found a part-time gardening job, it wasn't likely that he'd keep it for long. He's a kind man but almost as dependent in some respects as his mother.

Mum is 79. She can't walk on her own any more: she's got to be held up when she doesn't use the trolley (walker.) She needs to be lifted out of bed, washed, dressed, taken to the toilet... whenever she's in bed I have to help her onto the bucket.

It's the same every morning, even though I'm working now. I get up at six o'clock, give her her tablets and coffee and put some water on in the kitchen for it to be hot when the nurse arrives. I get the basin ready for her, towels, soap, comb, Mum's clothes... Then, up until I started work 3 days ago, I'd go shopping. We used to have lunch at the luncheon club together every day of the week. Now she has lunch with my sister and I take over after work. I only work part time. Mum has a nap until 4 or 5 in the afternoon. Then I stay here with her from 5 o'clock, all night until I leave for work the next morning. And also 24 hours a day Saturdays and Sundays, without the nurse to wash her at that.

Leisure time? Oh well,... I've got used to looking after my parents so much you know. I do take time off though, I go and see my sister who runs a cafe near by, I take a breath of fresh air, have a drink and a chat at the bar, have a bit of fun with my sister and my mates. I stay out for one, one and half hours, at the most, you never know what can happen.

A holiday? What for? I'm fine, here. Later maybe. But later means when she is.. Oh, well.. I've got this little job and if they keep me on I'll get a holiday anyway but.. yes, if something happens to her life will be different.. It will have to be, won't it? Most of all, I'll have to forget what I have lived through, won't I? I'll have to think about... when she dies, some time, all right.. I often think about it, actually.. it will be very hard, then. You should live with your parents, that's what you should do, because I value my parents a lot, I do.

Mum is no burden to me. She's not! It's only natural, your parents brought you up, it's only natural that you should look after them later, God knows how many people abandon their own parents, but those are barbarians, that's what they are; shouldn't be allowed to go on living. I'd rather have my mother here with me than put her in a hospital or workhouse or somewhere horrible like that ! My two sisters and my brother all appreciate what I do for her.

It's been four years, now. She used to stay with my sister, but it was too difficult, with her cafe to run and everything. My brother and sisters wanted to send her to hospital at some point. But I wouldn't have it! She was like she is now at the time. I refused to have her sent away and took her here with me. She lives at home, in her own house, in her own home... also, she's got her neighbours and everything. She said to me : "You must not let me go, son" So I said: "Don't worry, Mum, you won't go, you won't go to hospital, you'll be living in your own house and I'll take care of you."

Two people help me with the caring : the doctor next door and the nurse. Money is no problem. I already get a special care allowance, it's hardly 2,000 francs (303 ECU) per month mind you. Mum never worked, she brought her five children up, but she does get a little something from Dad's pension scheme, not much though. I used to get the social rehabilitation allowance. I don't know how much I'll be getting for that job of mine. The good thing is we don't pay any rent: Mum owns the house.

The municipality suggested I should take a house helper, but since I don't have a "job" - I only started one three days ago - I'd rather take care of her myself; also, looking after Mum means being with her for real. She is with me and that's that. We talk quite a bit, we watch TV together and everything... together.

I'll always look after her, even if she were to lose her mind. I'll do everything I can, I will!"

I LEARNED TO CARE THE HARD WAY

Maria lives in a relatively poor, once refugee area of central Athens with some state housing and many small blocks of flats. She is 56 years of age and looks after her 80 year old mother. There are five people living in the three roomed flat, her mother and father living in one room. Maria is married and her 25 year old daughter, who does not go out to work, still lives at home, though her son has married and moved away. They are a relatively low income family but the flat is comfortable and well furnished. While caring for her mother in her parents room she talked about her life as a carer.

"She's been 6-7 years in this state, paralysed on one side. It happened suddenly. She was then living in the village, which is an hour from Volos, but after the stroke she came to live here with us. While she was in hospital in Volos they wanted to cut her leg off but then she was transferred to the Hospital in Athens. She doesn't get out of bed. If she could get up there would be no problem. She hears well, but she has poor or no communication or understanding.

She is on insulin for her diabetes and has injections every morning. The hospital also gave her some other treatment. I gave her the tablets for 2-3 years then stopped since I didn't see any improvement. Now she just takes them for her circulation occasionally. I give her the injections; I've learned how. I take blood samples for examination and I also use test tapes for her urine. If her blood sugar is low I give her something sweet. She takes 27 units of insulin. The nurse told me what to do and I've learned over the past 6 years. We can't pay for help. One of my hands is useless. Her husband helps sometimes.

She complains and cries out all the time. She's had bed sores 2 or 3 times for which I've used medical powders. I've learned how to turn her. For the lavatory - well sometimes she tells me she wants to go, sometimes she has an accident. She has disposable napkins at night.

Sometimes she asks for the bedpan. Every Thursday I give her some senna tea and then take her to the toilet.

I had to learn to care for her. The most difficult problem is her weight - I'm 60 kilos and she's 80. I have to pull her this way and that to change the sheets, that's tiring enough. No one taught me, I learned the hard way. When a person can't look after themselves it's terrible. Of course others have the same problem but they die within a year. How did this happen to us? She is no better and no worse all these years, just the same. She had X-rays in the Hospital to see if she might improve but they just looked at them and shook their heads and said "Nothing can be done, her brain is very damaged".

My daily routine starts in the morning when I wash her top and bottom and comb her hair, give her insulin, bring her food. I spend about an hour with her, then into the kitchen for housework and cooking. She pees about 4/5 times a day. I give her food, running backwards and forwards from the kitchen. My father occupies her time - someone has to be with her. She shouts and wants company. She doesn't want TV. He tells her stories; she's like a child and it's the only thing that keeps her quiet.

There's me and my husband, my daughter and the old couple here in this flat. My son married and left. We have 3 rooms and my daughter has to sleep in the sitting room. We've been here in Athens many years but my parents came 6 years ago. We all go to the village house in the summer and take mother with us. My father helps and neighbours pop in and out. My mother will be with us till Easter then she'll go to stay with my brother till August, then we have a month in the summer in the village. My two brothers and I agreed on this rota of care. No one wants this sort of problem. Because my sister in law has small children, she takes her for less time but she also works so I go over regularly to her house when my mother is over there, to look after her while my sister in law is at work. She got herself some training so she could go out to work. Their bills don't come out right otherwise. I go over every morning and come back at lunchtime. There are other family members who would help if needed.

I wasn't working before my parents came to live with us I've worked hard enough in the past. My husband sells lottery tickets in the street. Mother shouts out at night, most nights and wakes us up. My husband hears her from the next room and says to me "Get up". They wanted to rent a separate house but couldn't find the money.

My mother has a pension of 50,000 drachmas (200 ECU) a month, 40,000 drachmas (160 ECU) invalidity pension and 10,000 drachmas (40 ECU) from OGA. The medical committee, neurologists and so on, came to assess her at home, she didn't have to go to them. My brother did all the papers for the pension.

She's not been in hospital since that first time. She has no personal doctor nearby, well not until now when we've enrolled her in the KAPI. Father was a member beforehand. Until now I had to go and get her insulin from the hospital. We have tried to rent a room and find a woman to help but there's not enough money to cover the costs. What other solutions are there? A hospital or an Old People's Home? The kids have suggested it but would it be OK? You hear a lot about them and it depends on the category; if you pay a lot they're better. As for other services there's nothing. My father got a hernia from lifting and they didn't even give him a belt. But someone else from the Local Authority clinic said get a belt and its helped him. He's too old for an operation. You just have to manage these things for yourself. Father can't help much and the others all moan. My mother in law wasn't bedridden and could still get about right up until she died three years ago.

We can only just manage like this, one on top of the other but we can't afford another room or to pay for help. We've discussed all other solutions, there's no other possibility. She could go on for years, God knows. Sometimes when she wakes at night and yells I think "My God, she's dying" but it's not in our hands. We just do what we can. Even if we could afford to put her in somewhere I'd still worry and it might be worse - in any case they don't take them when there in her state."

I AM HAPPY TO HAVE THEM ALL HERE WITH ME
BUT IT IS A MONOTONOUS LIFE

Beatrice, aged 63, lives in a rural village in the south of Portugal which is just beginning to change from traditional to more modern forms of agriculture. She and her husband have no children but live with their parents, Beatrice's mother, aged 88, and Manuel's parents - his mother is aged 91 and his father is 96 years old. This cohabitation began some years ago when their parents became dependent.

"My mother used to live a long way away. After the death of my father she lived on her own there until she fell and broke her leg. After that she couldn't stay alone any more and came to live with us. My husband's parents also lived in their own house in the village but gradually, as they got very old, they became more dependent and had to be taken care of. So they too came to live with us.

I'm resigned to the situation. During my life I've lived a lot with old and sick people so I'm familiar with it. My mother is very dependent on me. I have to wash and dress her. She walks with difficulty - she's got arteriosclerosis - so she needs me to help her; but she does eat by herself. When she's feeling well she can hold a conversation with me, but when she feels bad she sometimes gets very confused. She's much worse this past six months. I feel she's going from bad to worse.

My mother-in-law takes care of herself but my father-in-law needs someone to wash him. When he first came he could still walk but gradually his situation got worse. Now he can't wash himself and he has to use diapers. He's lost his sight too, but he can at least still eat by himself. He can't talk with us any more but he recognises his wife and his son.

I wake early in the morning, have my breakfast and serve breakfast to the others. Then I prepare lunch and go shopping. Once a week a housekeeper comes to clean the house. I take care of my mother and help her to wash and dress herself. My father-in-law has a bath only once a week. Except at weekends I have a daily home help for 3 hours in the morning and 2 hours in the afternoon. This girl helps me to take care of my father-in-law and she does what is necessary around the house. If I didn't have this help I suppose I could go on taking care of them all but I'd be forced to leave other things. Even now it's very difficult to go out because my mother is easily frightened.

I have thought about other ways of caring for them. The other solution would be an institution but they don't want to go there and as we can take care of them it's better to have them at home; at least they are with the family. I'm happy to have them here. If they went into an institution I wouldn't really like it. I wouldn't know if they were well or not. My mother-in-law is better than she was when she arrived here. In her own home she had to do everything for herself and its not easy for a person her age to go shopping, cook the meals and so on. Here she's much better off. She doesn't have to do anything. I prepare the meals and take care of everything. My father-in-law is also better here. They've someone to love and care for them.

Of course I'm frightened that they will become completely dependent, bedridden, because I just couldn't do everything alone. Even with the help during the day it still wouldn't be enough. And what about at night? Night help is very important. Not at the moment of course. It's not necessary now. However when my father-in-law first arrived he was incontinent and my mother-in-law didn't sleep at all. So we decided to use nappies. Before that we were always having to wash the linen, washing and washing - it wasn't any kind of life. Now he uses three nappies a day which works out very expensive every month but we use the money from his pension to buy them.

I don't really have any financial problems. We've got my own pension, my husband's pension, my mother's and my father-in-laws pensions. But what I really think I need is to have more home help. I need someone for about 8 hours a day and I don't have that at present.

I don't think I'd enjoy the idea of going away on holiday and leaving them because I wouldn't feel easy in my mind. But from time to time I do need to give myself a break. For example some time ago one of my husband's relatives died, it was in Chamusca, and we decided to go to the funeral. I had to make all the arrangements and eventually it needed 3 people to stay in our home to care for them all while I was away!

I don't really have any plans for the future; there's no joy in my life - it's just a monotonous life."

I WRITE ARTICLES FOR THE CARERS ASSOCIATION
TO TELL THEM WHAT THE TRUE SITUATION IS LIKE

Elizabeth (48) cares for her mother who is forty years older. Her mother is blind, bedridden and almost deaf. Elizabeth lives with her family and her mother in a middle-class, middle-income suburban estate in Dublin. The garden is well tended and her life is full - her own interests include painting and playing snooker and this gives her some respite from caring. However, while she has a strong sense of responsibility and love towards her mother, she is beginning to question her ability to care and is apprehensive that her own health will fail while her mother still requires care.

"All her life my mother had good health but about 8 or 9 years ago her sight began to fail; she's now totally blind and has become feeble as well. She's blind, bedridden and practically deaf, she's not able to do anything for herself and is very embarrassed about her condition. Her theory is that the family should look after their own. She would be very agitated at the thought of any stranger coming next or near her room. The way I see it, there's a very thin border line decision to make - "where does duty stop?". There was a great deal of agonizing over this particular problem, it wasn't a free choice - I was simply landed with the job as there was no one else to do it.

I've been very lucky in the fact that she fitted in so well. My husband and children idolise her and she loves children. I find it's good for the children to have an older person living in the house as it gives them an idea of an older generation. At times I feel I might be taking advantage of them and at this point in their lives they need as much time as they can to study.

I get great support from my sister in law - she gives me great psychological help. Margaret's visits to me always give me a great lift. I consider her a very sensible and understanding person and if

I've a problem or don't know how to handle something she always has the right answer. Her support is marvellous. Also the Public Health Nurse has become a friend, I've been very lucky, and she comes once a week. If I'm feeling down she makes me see it all in a different light and she has been wonderful in the support that she's given me.

One thing that is really difficult is that my mother has a real problem with incontinence; for that reason there's a lot of work and expense with sheets, laundry and so on. If there's a queue in the launderette I become panicky as I haven't got time to spare as anything could happen even when I'm out for those few short minutes. When I go shopping I'm constantly looking at the time. She's fallen a few times and I'm very anxious when I leave her.

I love the joy of putting paint on canvas and for me it's a great hobby. I used to go to a very good class and that gave me great joy but I had to give up the painting class to become a carer as I couldn't be away for 3 hours. I purchased a small snooker table and find this very relaxing - just to occupy an hour. At night or in the evening it's a great way of diffusing stress.

It's a very difficult situation for my mother and everyone involved and I'm very sorry about that. It's a problem and what I have to do as carer is minimise it. For instance, she has never seen one of my paintings - she knows I sell them. So I always bring up completed paintings, let her feel the canvas and explain exactly what the painting is, so she's not missing out on it all. She gets a mental picture of it and that makes for normality.

I'm always afraid that my health will break down at some stage. I can never say what will happen, I just try to take one day at a time. I'm OK today but tomorrow I might be in deep depression. However I can't allow my depression to show; also there's a fear of a slipped disc if I'm trying to lift her and I'm not fully trained in what to do. I write articles for magazines to do with caring for the Carer's Association. I tell them what the true situation is really like and it helps me a lot too because I can share these feelings with every other Carer in Ireland.

There is no way I can have a holiday, I have to remain in the house. I haven't left Dublin for a long-term holiday for 8 or 9 years. I haven't taken a weekend break either as my mother won't tolerate a stranger in the house. I have gone on day trips for a couple of hours with a friend and that's my holiday! There is no question of putting her in a home, even in the short term. Surroundings are very important to my mother, familiar sounds for instance milk bottles on the door step. To be removed from that environment would be a totally traumatic experience.

My mother is blind and bedridden and people ask 'Is she mobile?' They just can't seem to understand she's blind and bedridden and if she stood up she'd fall over. People say "Oh, you're very good", "You'll have your reward in the next world", but I'd like my reward now. People say I'm great but I'm not, I can't give her the professional nursing skills, like the Public Health Nurses can; with me it's just hit and miss. I make her as comfortable as I can. But as for the mechanics of nursing, I'm no good at that. It's just a job that has to be done, I'm no saint."

IT'S ONLY WHEN I SEE THE KNITTING THAT I'VE DONE
THAT I KNOW I EXIST

Francoise is 52 and lost her job a year ago. Her husband, Roland, 62, has just retired. They have three daughters; the older two are married with young children and both working; one of them lives next door. The youngest is now finishing her studies in Rennes and comes home for the weekends and holidays. They live in a small Breton town of 10,000 inhabitants and own their small but comfortable home. Though not wealthy, they are not in financial difficulties and her parents now live with them. Over the past two years her father, aged 77, has been weakened by serious health problems and a series of operations, and is nearly blind; he also suffers from intermittent urinary incontinence and mental disorders. Her mother, 75, is afflicted with senile dementia; both parents walk with difficulty. Francoise used to look after her mother-in-law who also lived with the couple when she was ill and convalescing.

"I have to do everything for both of them; give them medicines, bring them food, butter their bread even, dress them... they can feed themselves. After his last stroke we thought Dad would never manage it again but he did. Eating takes ever so long. Mum eats very slowly, so the table remains set for a very long time for each meal. That's a pain in the neck.

Dad has just come out of the hospital - last Monday or Tuesday. So there is a nurse coming to wash him every morning. At the moment that is; I don't know how long she'll be coming for. Mum can just about manage to wash herself, provided you watch over her, 'cause if you don't.. Look, she finished dressing just now, she put on everything inside out, she put her dress on and her nightie on top. The other day she put her slip on her head for a hat. She wants almost constant supervision; she can be up to anything, any time. I have to shut everything up: knives, medicines, chemicals, bottles, you name it! She may leave the lavatory brush on the chest of drawers or some used nappy on the table, wet side down on the wood, of course; or turn the bath taps on; I even found the gas bottle tap turned on once! I sometimes think that she does it knowingly. Maybe just to attract my attention.

I always stay home nowadays. Permanently. I'm not working any more; I couldn't with two people like that on my hands anyway. I was quite happy when I was made redundant; I had too much to do altogether but I realise that I miss my workmates and I miss going out. Officially I'm still looking for a job... well, I don't expect to find one, considering my age, but I'd like to go back to the factory if I could. I don't go out any more at all be it for the sake of it or to do the shopping. My husband has been doing the shopping for us since he retired. I do go out to the hairdresser's or the doctor's when I have to, naturally, but it's always a matter of running there and back. My husband is supposed to stay here when I go out but he doesn't always. Dad is in bed most of the time with his arthritis and many health problems. But Mum can be up to the most unimaginable kinds of mischief as soon as she thinks I'm not looking. She searches every room, turns the place upside down and I end up finding things in the most ludicrous places... if I do ever find them again, that is. Not easy, eh? Also she tries to find the bottles... I wonder if she doesn't drink when I'm not watching. One of them does, only we're not sure who yet...

My parents used to live just across the street, which was quite handy for me when their health started failing, but then Dad kept falling ill and he had to be operated on again and again so naturally both of them came to live here with us each time he was recovering. Mum couldn't really be left on her own whenever Dad was in hospital because she was becoming senile. But my husband and I were still working, it wasn't easy as you can imagine. Dad was just about bedridden and couldn't supervise her properly, so sometimes, after work, ...oh dear! what a mess! You just can't imagine!!

They did have a house-helper from the Welfare Department coming to clean the house and the Department also had an alarm switch installed in their house. It was for Dad to use because he had huge health problems and couldn't speak or write after his stroke but somehow his brain could still function, so if there was anything wrong he could ring for help. These helps stopped when Mum and Dad came to live here with us. Except for the nurse who's been coming for the last three days... but how long will that last?

The good thing about the alarm is that I could be sure that as long as the welfare people didn't ring me up at the factory, everything was fine. Nevertheless I'd keep fretting about actually getting a phone call because whenever I did I had to run to my parents' house straight away, never mind work. So I was also afraid they'd sack me because of this. When the company started having problems I was in the first batch that got fired, needless to say. At least, I thought, I'd be able to look after these two better, which is true, but did it solve anything all the same? Now that I'm shut off in here and don't see anybody any more... I've come to wonder, you know?

What was it I wanted to tell you? Oh yes, about the nurses and washing my father. How shall I put it?... If only it were just a matter of washing his face and trunk and legs even, I'd be all right,.. but... his private parts!.. Do you get my meaning? I just can't. (Whispering) Once he.. he.. what came over him I don't know. Did he have a memory lapse or did he not realise what he was doing? Anyway, he took my hand and .. there was sperm everywhere. So after that, as far as I am concerned, his penis... Oh no! Washing him is just too awkward for me. What will happen if the health service stops providing a nurse after a short while?

My husband is at home all the time now. When he was working it was all right because he was out in the daytime and he didn't bring any - how shall I put it? .. pressure to bear, if that's what you call it. Anyway, I've noticed that since he's retired.. he's starting to have health troubles that may or may not last long.. That'll be another one for me to look after, won't it?... well I should hope not! Anyway, he's been less thoughtful lately, less - words fail me too sometimes - ..

less patient, a bit aggressive, irritable. That's because, you've got to understand him - it's a difficult time people go through when they retire: giving up their jobs, finding themselves.. They know they must not look back. They know perfectly well - so what -? They end up more or less waiting... waiting for what? they don't know. Retirement is totally different from working life. People know it, but this doesn't mean that they manage to get themselves organised. It takes a while, and it's been only a few months since my husband retired. On top of this, with my parents living with us, we've had to forget about quite a few things we meant to do when we retired. This is no easy situation for him either. Between you and me, he did have serious problems at one time. He'd say: "I can't stand this any more!!" And it was as bad for me: whenever I tended my parents he couldn't stand it and whenever I looked after him they couldn't stand it, so I was always caught up between him, my daughter, my other daughter, my grandchildren, my parents: they were all getting at me, out of some kind of rivalry and jealousy of one another. None of them ever thinks of me. On the contrary they keep calling my attention to themselves all the time. That's why I think to myself :"I must escape", but how?

My husband does try to help, doing the shopping and things, he can keep away from the house then, like he does when he goes to those meetings of his. He can go out, I can't. He's a man of goodwill, but... a man all the same, not a woman, a woman is more aware of other people's needs. A man could never replace a woman, be it only as far as affection goes.

On top of everything else, some evenings or at weekends, often as early as Friday night, my grand children come too. I often baby-sit for my daughter and her husband so they can go out and enjoy themselves a bit. They work all week, you see. I also do all the housework. There's quite a bit to do there too! I leave some of it... I only do what's most urgent nowadays. Like my daughter's washing: she's away in Rennes all week and comes home at weekends bringing her dirty washing with her. I usually have hardly two days to wash, dry and iron all her clothes; trousers, skirts, God knows how many T-shirts. And when she's here, whatever I do there's a.. generation gap problem as well. You manage to ignore some things because its your own child of course, but sometimes.. it gets too much. But you have to cope with it all the same, don't you?

My family doctor keeps saying to me : "Think of yourself! Please!" The doctor in charge of my father at the hospital said to me :"Why on earth won't you send him to a nursing home, huh?" The thing is, Mum's retirement pension is tiny and Dad doesn't get much either as an ex-miner. So it's just impossible given the amount those places charge you. Besides there are two of them and I'm an only child! I heard that they charge you according to the type of care a patient requires: now there are three different categories of care and my parents would necessarily fall into the third one, which means a minimum charge of 7000 Francs monthly!! PER PERSON! (1060 ECU) It's just impossible! Just think, it would land up at 15,000 Francs a month which is as much as Dad gets quarterly. Some people told me that in cases like mine you can get government aid, but I think that they'll pester me for the money back eventually. The government even takes money off people's grandchildren! That means that my own children will have to pay for it, won't they? I won't have it! As long as I can make it, as long as I'm still standing, I'll go on. Life is difficult enough for young people as it is, they don't want that kind of thing on top of everything else, do they?

Mum and Dad get a 100% health service refund on their medical expenses - I think so anyway. I was told that the health service is paying for the nurse and for the hospital bed that had to be brought here. But because it's only been here a few days, I don't have any details.

Apart from that, I don't get any help. Neither financial nor from the family or anything. No help with the washing, cleaning, supervising and so on, none, none at all. But as long as I can face this work load, I'll face it. Now if I were on my own and had to go out, if only to do the shopping, I couldn't make it.

If I wanted to escape for a while, when my husband is at home, I could, if he were willing to watch over them. What I miss the most is a holiday. We could escape for a while, my husband and I, if we could take some time off. But I'm well aware it's impossible because we can't leave these two on their own. Apart from that it's not too bad because we never went out much, we don't engage in any sort of hobby, especially me. My husband used to cycle, but he stopped when he got heart trouble. However he does go to his club; I used to be a member too but I left because of my parents. One thing you do need when you're busy all year round is a holiday. To take a breather. We did manage to get away last year though for how long, I don't remember, it seems so far back - but not just the two of us, unfortunately; we took my daughter's eldest son with us. We left my parents in a special home that takes in old people while their children are on holiday. But this year I don't know what we can do with Dad, with his being in such a state. Mum could go but Grandad couldn't. They don't provide medical care in those places, you see. They'd need someone staying with them here 24 hours a day, but I can't imagine anyone willing to do everything I do. I don't think there are organizations that provide help for people like me who need to take a break, I don't think there are any. If only we could take two weeks off! Just two weeks! I'm not even asking for 4 weeks like everybody else gets; no less than two, though. One week is too short, really, it's not worth it. If I only could have two weeks off!

So one day you just break down, don't you? You can't think why that particular day, and not the day before. One tiny thing goes wrong and you go beserk... Why? I ask you. You just don't know why. When your child does something wrong you just smack it, don't you? But when it's your own mother or father doing something wrong, it would be frowned upon if.. you happened to ... But sometimes you just lose control, you get into a temper... or get violent even, sometimes your hand just goes, you don't realise it. You regret it straight away of course, but.. oh, dear! .. to realise what you've done, raising a hand to your own parents! Oh no!

I had another nervous breakdown a while ago and I'm still taking tablets so I can sleep and calm down. I go through times when I can feel I'm quite brittle. There are always more or less serious clashes with two people like them around, relationships are always tense. I'm prone to depression I know I am. I'm prone to depression and sometimes I feel that it would take very little to make me go beserk. Like Monday last, when Dad came back from hospital; I'd cleaned everything, the whole house through and through, put clean sheets on their bed, disinfected everything with bleach, all for Dad's return from hospital.. I took a lot of trouble over it, I really did... So when I saw what he'd done I.. oh! I could have... I screamed: "What have you done? I put everything there for you, I put the bucket there precisely for you to relieve yourself in !" So he said: "You poor thing, I just didn't take the hint and I can hardly see anything, anyhow." You see, this situation isn't easy for any of us. We all suffer from it. He does too, I'm sure. Maybe that's why he has since been trying to get out of bed to go to the toilet, although he can hardly stand.

I try to bear it and keep quiet, or make things sound nicer because we can't speak freely. Does he understand what we say? What about her? That's why my husband and I can have no intimacy any more, be it in conversation or otherwise. They occupy our bedroom and we sleep in here on the sofa, in the middle of the lounge. Our clothes, our things are all scattered around the house, upstairs, downstairs. God knows where. When they are both sleeping and I need to get something from the bedroom I daren't go in in case I disturb them, so I wait.

I also have a problem when I think to myself:"What shall I be like when I grow old?" It's a problem too, you automatically ask yourself "Shall I become like that? Maybe I'll be even worse!" You think of it a lot and it makes you confront the generation gap as well. "How will my children react?" you ask yourself. You can't tell yourself any more "Let's not think about it, we'll see." You can't take it light heartedly any more when you have so many problems with your parents. It's not palpable, but it isn't science fiction either, it's just concrete everyday life.

Maybe I bore you with all my troubles. I go on and on.. I'd never told anyone all this before. I don't mean to complain but you're doing a survey, aren't you? You want people to know what's going on, well, the carer is the one who knows and must speak out for everyone to know. Everyone must know that caring is about forgetting about everything, forgetting about one's life, forgetting about oneself. I know that now, but I couldn't have imagined it before, not in a life time. My daughters say to me : "Please, Mum, think of yourself! You think of other people all the time". The thing is I can't, I don't have time to think of myself. I'm constantly worried and tense, constantly starting things all over again. My doctor was saying to me :"Find something to do just for yourself, go out, do something, anything, but please take your mind off everything." As it happened I found something that suits me without looking - knitting! I forget everything else when I'm knitting. When I have a back ache or any kind of ache.., or whatever, I start knitting and I forget it. It gets on my husband's nerves but never mind. If I don't spend some time knitting I get the impression that I'm not living, that I don't... When I'm knitting I just exist! You see all my life is about waiting on everyone else, cooking, washing up, cleaning the house and so on, and all this leaves no trace, does it? It's always got to be done all over again, nothing positive ever comes out of it, nothing palpable, nothing is ever achieved, do you understand what I mean? The good thing about knitting is that I can actually see what I have done, I can actually see where my time went. When my husband fixes something he actually sees the result: when he paints a wall he sees what he's done; when he plants something he sees it grow. But what I do leaves no trace at all, except my knitting: I do something and it stays done. It's only when I see the knitting I've done that I know I exist."

CARING FOR MY WIFE IS A MATTER OF LOVE

Juanito is the companion of Modesta. Both are seventy five years old and have lived together for almost fifty years. They were never able to get married because he was already married and divorce did not exist then. A few months ago Modesta fell ill with heart problems and since then Juanito has taken care of her and the house. Their only daughter lives in a city some distance away, is separated with three small children and cannot be of great help. Several years ago the couple moved from the city of Barcelona to the village, where they had inherited a house. Juanito talks about caring for the woman he loves.

"In this village everybody knows each other; you go out in the street and nobody is a stranger, we are all locals. From the moment Modesta got sick people come to the house all the time, they even come from Barcelona to see her. We came to live here some five years ago because it's easier to live here.

Currently my wife depends totally on me. She has been sick for several months and she will never be able to live a normal life any more. I go shopping. I have to make her food, the bed and meet all her needs. In this village there is a lot of co-operation and help, more than in the city. It is a supportive environment but I haven't needed any help yet. When she became sick I had to enter the kitchen for the first time ever. I have learned to cook, but that is easy. I take care of her diet and make her meals with very little salt. I also go shopping for groceries and really like it. I used to be a merchant, going out and seeing people stimulates me and I feel people like me better than before, now that I look after my wife.

Before, when she was fine, I used to get up first in the morning, have breakfast and make breakfast for her. When it was ready I woke her up. One day I'd call her in Spanish, another in German, another in English - and she knew breakfast was on the table. But since she became ill she has breakfast later, so I go shopping first, do the dishes from the day before, and when I've finished everything I bring her the drugs and breakfast.

At the beginning I had to help her in her personal hygiene, it was the most difficult moment when she did everything on herself. It was very unpleasant when I had to clean her but I did it anyway and I preferred to do it myself rather than a nurse. I felt responsible for her. I try to be more loving than before because I can tell that she needs it but even before that I was a loving person. The problem she has now is in feeling diminished next to me and not being able to give me the same care I give her. She feels handicapped and it's very traumatic for her. Modesta is an intelligent person, responsible, and she knows that she will never be able to be the same as before.

I cannot accept anybody else doing the job I do for my wife, I am the one who must do it, because that is the marriage commitment. It also pleases me to fulfil such an obligation, if you scratch a little bit you might find some egoism in my behaviour! I am in general very disappointed with life but I believe people owe each other debts, and sometimes we forget that. When you remember it is nice, it is a kind of defence against modern life in which everyone is on his own doing things only for himself. For that reason to dedicate yourself to others is like paying a price in life, because with our individualism we are hurting ourselves. That is why altruistic activities are carried out for their own sake, but it is a beneficial selfishness.

Caring for my wife is a matter of love. The reason is very simple. I do for her what I would like her to do for me, it is very elementary. I undertake the care of my wife as an unconscious impulse, it is like a natural instinct that makes us human. In what I feel for my wife, the gratitude, the sexual attraction, the mutual affinity and fondness, the life together for forty five years are all added together. I will always be grateful to her for believing in my word when we met and she was a single woman and I was married. I could not offer her anything because her economic situation was better than mine. She left everything to come with me without any guarantee of security because being a married man I could not get married again. The most traumatic ordeal of all is the fear of losing her.

Now I have much less free time than before. For me, free time is when you stop doing things you are obliged to in order to do others that are distracting. It is a need as well as a right that people look forward to having free time. Now I have fewer hours, but I still do the activities I like: read, walk around, watch TV, play chess, I just keep doing everything the same way.

Nobody talks about the sexual life of people who get older, and it is very important. To me that is a big problem. We lived a normal sexual life until my wife got sick. Now that I experience it I realize the magnitude of the problem, before I never thought about it. This is probably the most problematic aspect since my wife got sick; it is not really serious yet because it is recent, but with the passing of time it will become more serious. I do not know how to resolve it, it is an annoyance. My wife feels it is also her biggest problem, she knows she cannot satisfy me, and there is still plenty of attraction between us.

We have not been taught to accept death, it is something that affects us a lot when it touches someone you love. I worshipped my mother, I loved her more than anything else in the world, and I still love her. I was present when she died, in that very instance that body was not my mother any more, it revolted me and I wanted to bury her fast. So when death arrived the most important things were the memories, the teachings, what she represented, all I made her suffer, the happiness we shared, not the physical part. That body was not my mother any more. My mother is still alive in me and many days I dream about her.

If I got sick it would be a major problem. In this village there is nobody to take care of us, there are no doctors or nurses, only the good relations between the people. In a serious case it is the only solution. In this town there are old people living alone, both men and women. In cases where they need help, the neighbours take care of it.

Sometimes when they get very old and can't take care of themselves some relatives take them. The other day a neighbour tried to commit suicide, he was sick, got depressed and tried to commit suicide by gas.

I am concerned about my own ageing. Sometimes I think the solution might be to commit suicide. It is a thought that comes to my mind when I see an old person in bad shape, not enjoying life. It is more beautiful to look for death than to wait for death to come looking for you and in the meantime being affected by that senile dementia that prevents you from making decisions."

I STRUGGLE ON ALONE

Petros has been looking after his invalid wife, Popi, for the past 15 years. She is 75 while he is 84 years of age. She became hemiplegic following a stroke and is paralysed in her left arm and leg. Since then she's had another stroke which has affected her sight so that she is almost blind. The two of them live with their mentally disturbed and dependent son in a two and a half roomed, first floor flat in an inner urban area of Athens. We leave Petros to talk about his life and problems as a carer:

"Look at all those medicines! In 1977 she had her first stroke, suddenly one day, on her left side. For 6 years she didn't get up at all. I brought a professor, a very good doctor, to see her: he gave her Aslan injections, 1200 altogether to try and get her up. He said to be patient, just be patient, injections morning and night, year after year; but after seven years she finally got out of bed and now she can move around a bit in the flat. So many injections! Now she takes all these pills, eight a day, day after day and I take her blood pressure.

Sunday, a month ago I got her up to go to the loo, she says "I can't see" so I called the ambulance for the hospital. They examined her and said "She's had another stroke". They said she should be admitted since she had to rest, but I would have had to pay 5000 a day (20 ECU) for a special nurse to look after her: who else would look after her? I don't have any money, I'm a pensioner and I've only got 30,000 drachmas (120 ECU) a month from TEBE. (pension fund) It's nothing. So I brought her home and put her to bed here. It's a month since she had that stroke. As far as her eyes are concerned the hospital said she'd get her sight back gradually.

I struggle on alone. She can get up a bit. I get her up. She can go to the loo with my help. She can't see at all. I'm ill too, I was in hospital 5 months ago with intestinal obstruction. This was in

September when I went in and I stayed there for virtually 2 months. I had an operation then I had to wear a belt. Just one more problem. The flat caretaker's wife looked after her to some extent while I was away. As soon as I got out, a month later she had the second stroke. The same thing all over again, again and again.

I cook, we've no money, nothing. I do everything. I take the sheets and laundry to the launderette and pay 1000 drachmas, (4 ECU) and the underclothes I wash by hand and put out to dry. I go out for a bit to shop for food and come home again. We've only one child and he's ill.

I had two older sisters who died and now I've nobody. My wife is from Larissa but that's far away; she has two sisters - but nobody comes to visit although we used to go there 15-20 years ago.

The Red Cross Gerontological Service worker has been coming for the past 10 years to visit us and she takes our blood pressure. We learned about this service from the neighbours; it's nearby. They told me about this lady and I went and found her and brought her here. She looked at my wife and she took her blood pressure and sent some other girls. Since then occasionally they bring food and stuff. And so the years have passed but I've suffered a lot, really a lot.

Medicines we get on our insurance book TEBE/IKA. They used to give them with a 90% reduction but they cut that and now we have to pay more. I went today to get the medicines and they cost 5500 drachmas (22 ECU), and of that I'll give about 2,000 drachmas (8 ECU) to the chemist.

We use the IKA insurance doctor. I make an appointment and they write a prescription. It's the IKA Clinic at Panathanaikos, if you know where that is? I need one or 2 buses to get there. I go at 6.00am. We used to go and wait our turn; there could be a 100 people in the queue. Now I phone - 10 days ago I phoned for an appointment at 7.00 am - they opened at 7.15 am. Now you go by appointment. The system works one month with queues and one month with appointments! The doctor wrote the prescription and I'll go again tomorrow to get it from the pharmacy.

The doctor knows me, he's been to see my wife at home. He takes money for home visits but he doesn't take much from me. He's a black foreign doctor who lives here about. We know one another. He's a very good chap and a good doctor. He's been here three or four times. He usually charges 7000 but takes 3000 drachmas (12 ECU) from me and I can phone him in an emergency. But this isn't an acute illness, it's a long term problem, endless, and it won't improve because her arm and leg have become deformed and immobile.

I can just about get her up to go to the bathroom, I wash her and wash her hair too. I do everything. She has a wheelchair that the service gave us, but it's no help since I can't get her out in it. She's been inside for 15 years continuously. I go out a bit, mainly to the shops and to get the medicines, but I rush back in case she's fallen down. Who will take her to the toilet if I'm not here? I take her. In the night perhaps 6/7 times she may want to get up to wee because the medicines have this effect. I take her at 1 o'clock, 2 o'clock, 4 o'clock...oh, God, not again ! I don't sleep.

For 6 years she didn't get up at all and I used to feed her in bed. Now I get her up and she can eat at the table. But because her hands don't work I still have to feed her, and also she can't see.

In the neighbourhood we used to have people who helped and visited but people get tired. For five and six years they were around, but they got fed up after so many years, as did our relatives- it's a long term problem.

She hasn't been in any other hospital or institutions. She can't go into a clinic because she must have a woman (a private nurse) to look after her full time. The nursing staff can't spend all their time with one person, so you need 5000 drachmas (20 ECU) in the morning and 5000 for the night shift. That's impossible for us financially so I endure it all at home. Even the TV is broken.

I had a grocer's shop which I shut in 1970 when I became ill and I have a small pension from that. Fortunately it's our own house - 2 rooms.

But with only 30,000 (120 ECU) drachmas a month from the pension what can I do ? We need money for the bills - 10,000 drachmas for DEH (electricity), 7000 drachmas a month for the flat maintenance and heating. The money just won't go round. We get enough food if we have the money, otherwise we go without. My wife needs various things. She gets a small disability allowance. We applied to the Ministry, they examined her - we took her with the ambulance, and the Committee saw her. That was seven or eight years ago when she was really bad. We learned about the allowance from the Red Cross lady, she helped with the papers. Unfortunately it's not just for 1 or 2 years which would be bearable but 10 years hard work, caring day in and day out."

I'M MORE LIKE HIS MUM NOW THAN HIS WIFE

Edith and Jorgen live in their own house where the family shop is based in a provincial town in Zeeland, Denmark. Edith, who is 70 years old, has been looking after her husband, aged 73, for five years now and expects her care situation at home to be replaced at some time by a move into a nursing home. But she will keep going for as long as is necessary.

"I seem to have spent most of my adult life looking after other people. Children, my mother, and now Jorgen. We'd been looking forward to our retirement, had made so many plans, and then this happens. As if having to look after him wasn't enough, I had to start looking after the shop as well. I'd never worked before that, just been the loving mother and wife and daughter. But he started going down hill - now he's very dependent on me and suffers from severe dementia - so I had to take over the shop so that we could stay in this house. At least we don't have to worry about money, not yet at least, but at some stage I won't be able to cope with it all and then the shop and house will have to go I suppose. As long as I can cope, I don't need help.

But I do worry. There's a lot to worry about too. The shop, the house, Jorgen, the future. I've never felt this insecure before. It helps talking to others. It's nice to talk to someone about it and everyone is very understanding, but they don't really know what it's like. You don't know until you're in the middle of it and then there's no time to think whether you can cope. You have to cope, don't you?

We do get a lot of help I suppose. Not financially, but then again that's not necessary. There's one or two special fittings in the bathroom and Jorgen goes along to the day-centre every day. That means I can look after the shop without having to worry about him, what he's doing. Some days he doesn't know what he's doing and doesn't know me even. It makes me sad to see him like that. I'm more like his Mum now than his wife.

Of course I couldn't give up on him now, not when he needs me most of all. He can still dress and wash himself most of the time. I don't know very much about dementia and it would be nice to have something I could read. I've fetched one or two leaflets from the library, but there wasn't a lot in them. It's difficult sometimes to know what is normal, the way he is, what I should expect. And I get upset if I get angry.. he can't help it.

Our life now is quite restricted. The weekdays are pretty much the same, he's away at the day centre and I'm in the shop and have to do what has to be done around the house. Weekends I'm busy keeping him occupied, keeping him out of trouble. We don't get out much at all. We've no car and it's too much of a job with the bus. The children fetch us sometimes for a visit but it's all so much trouble. It's easier just to stay here. i would like a holiday, on my own though. Is that awful? If I could be sure he was OK, it would do us both a world of good.

My husband must be as happy as he can be, but when it becomes impossible to look after him, I don't want to be martyr."

I WAS ABLE TO SAY GOODBYE TO HIM IN OUR OWN FAMILAR SURROUNDINGS

Mrs. Boonstra is an energetic seventy year old woman whose husband (75) died of cancer of the pancreas a few months before the interview after a short illness. Their home is a large villa in a town in the south of Holland. Their seven children are all grown up and have left home. Only one of them still lives in the same town. Mrs. Boonstra did not have to worry about money and with the ample pension of her husband and good, medical insurance they could also hire a private nurse.

"I'll never forget the moment when the doctor - in the hall, believe it or not, where he was constantly being interrupted, bluntly told us that my husband was incurably ill and that they couldn't do anything for him at the hospital. I'm still angry that the doctor did that in such an incredibly rude way. He also hadn't informed our GP that my husband was discharged from hospital. When, a few days later, I phoned our GP to ask about my husband's diet, he knew nothing about it.

When I learnt that my husband had only a few months to live I knew straightaway that I'd take him home and care for him myself. This was also what he wanted most. The fact that I was going to care for him at home was a matter of course for me. My husband had explicitly asked me to do so, because he thought the hospital was much too impersonal and he didn't want to lie there for months. Though I knew it was going to be a tough job, because he wasn't going to get well again and, what's more, he doesn't express his feelings very easily, I never doubted my decision. Even when it became more difficult I definitely didn't want to let him go to hospital. Fortunately I'm a person who knows how to set about things and moreover I used to be a nurse myself before my marriage. But the fact that it would be so exhausting emotionally to see your husband become terribly ill and a completely emaciated person in such a short time was something I'd not expected. Physically it wasn't too hard, though my back was giving me trouble and, at a certain point, my arms were full of bruises because I had to turn and lift him.

But emotionally it was especially hard even though I received a lot of support from my children. Well, I was the only one who was on the job night and day. Moreover he depended on me a lot, I was his prop, the only one he could cling to during this ruthless deterioration process over which he had no control.

Initially my husband was able to be out of bed regularly and he could still eat and drink, though moderately and with the greatest possible effort. But after a few weeks it was too tiring for him to dress and undress himself and climb the stairs. So we bought a special bed and put it in his study. At first he only slept there during the day but after about seven weeks - he was put on a drip by then - it became too dangerous to take him upstairs, even when there were two people to help. He was so weakened that he could collapse at any moment and if we tumbled down the three of us it would be a real disaster. My greatest fear was that I too would be put out of commission. Because if I wouldn't be available full-time any more - after all I was the pivot around whom everything revolved - how would we be able to keep my husband at home till the end? I must admit it took a long time before I called in professional help. I wanted to do it myself so badly and I knew that my husband wouldn't like too many strangers around the house. But on the advice of my GP I called in the district nursing services after about six weeks. From that moment on someone came to wash him and change his clothes every morning. This had really become a tough job that I couldn't do any more, even with the help of one of my children, because his stomach, which was terribly swollen, was in the way and as we weren't used to doing these kind of things we were hurting him needlessly, though he never complained about it. He never complained during all the three months but was awfully grateful for everything we did for him. It was almost painful when he said 'thank you' so often, because we were so glad that there was something we could do for him. At first we were able to do the necessary things for him even if it was only preparing food he liked, rubbing his dry lips or bedsores with ointment, changing his drip bags or putting a sheepskin under him. But in the end there were less things we could do for him and this gnaws away at you. Very often I became angry and rebellious.

In itself I was very satisfied with the district nurses, they were nice girls, but we didn't have a regular nurse. This annoyed me just as much as the fact that they didn't come at the same time everyday. So, at the insistence of my children, I called in a private nursing agency after eight weeks. From that moment on there was a nurse every night, so that I was able to get my night's rest. I'd chosen the private nursing agency because I'd heard good things about them; you could choose the nurses yourself and if there was one we didn't approve of or if my husband couldn't get along with her then we could ask for someone else. But this wasn't necessary. All that period the same two nurses came to us and my husband got attached to them. I've nothing but praise for this nursing agency. When, in the end, I needed a day nurse I only had to call and somebody came straightaway. Besides, my medical insurance paid for it.

The person who was a great support to me was our GP. At a time like that it becomes apparent how important a good GP is. You could call him night and day and even when he had weekends off he was prepared to come, like when my husband was short of breath. When there were moments when I didn't know what to do he came round, sometimes even twice a day. He gave both of us the feeling that he would never let us down, that he would do everything within his power to keep my husband at home.

My husband experienced these three months at home as a great gift. Surrounded by attention, care and love, from his seven children too; very often he couldn't believe this was happening to him. He felt very happy that all his children were ready to help him and wanted to care for him, he hadn't quite expected this. Partly because of this he kept up the fight longer than everybody had expected. It has to be said, all my children - and it surprised me too that there was no one who backed out - came to help when it was needed. No matter how busy they were with their own children or jobs and no matter how far away they lived, they came at least once every ten days, and my oldest and youngest daughters even more often. Anyhow, there was always one of them in the evenings and at night during the last few weeks because when after a few weeks it turned out that he was becoming worse very rapidly my eldest daughter (42) took it upon herself to organise a rota. My children had to tell her who would come when to support me and to lend a helping hand. This worked out very well. There were only a few nights and days during the last six weeks when I had to cope on my own. The presence of my children was a great support to me, especially mentally. When they were there I could cry and vent my feelings because when I was with my husband I wanted to put on a brave face. Taking care of him at home for three months took a lot of energy, but I'm glad that I was healthy enough to be able to do it all. I was able to say goodbye to him in our own familiar surroundings. The bond between me and my children and sisters has also become stronger because of this. I also noticed that the bond between my children has become much stronger. This is quite an unexpected consequence of such a difficult period. Though I kept saying that I could cope physically, looking back it's been an attack on my health. Apart from losing fourteen kilos during that period, I've been sickly on and off these past months since he died, whereas I never used to be ill before. Now I keep on having colds or the 'flu."

I STILL HAVE ENOUGH TIME FOR MYSELF

Hans is 78 and worked as an engineer until he retired. For the last four years he has been looking after his wife (77) who suffers from Alzheimer's disease. The couple live in their own house with garden in a large German city. One of their two daughters lives in the same house but they have little contact with her. The other daughter lives with her family on the outskirts of Hamburg and the son-in-law is the couple's GP.

Hans started by describing a typical day in his life as a carer:

"I get up at half past seven, get myself washed and dressed, go for rolls and prepare breakfast, which is ready about half past eight. Then I get my wife up, fetch her to the breakfast table in her dressing gown. Breakfast takes her a long, long time, till around half past nine. Then I change her diapers. After this I wash and dress her. Then she has a rest until midday. At twelve o'clock I start making lunch.

My wife is on the heavy side, she weighs nearly 100 kilos. She doesn't even eat that much - it's the lack of movement that does it. She used to be very sporty and was in good shape. Some years ago she had a biliary complaint and had to have an operation, which cured it. But the doctors reckon that the anaesthetic brought on the Alzheimer's disease. She takes 20 drops of medicine twice a day for it, to stimulate the blood circulation through the brain. No other treatment is required, as there's little that can be done. You can slow down the destruction of the brain cells but you can't actually stop it.

For some years now a cleaning lady has been coming once a week for three and a half hours to clean the flat. I don't have any other medical or nursing assistance. Our GP is our son-in-law; thank's to him I'm well informed and my daughter too. For example it was they who applied for the new attendance allowance. I was informed and they organised it. So as far as illnesses are concerned we have my son in law and now there's my granddaughter who is studying medicine and always bombarding me with bits of advice, which I'm not so keen on, but she means well. Somehow I don't feel the need to talk to friends or specialists.

With regard to organisations which offer support to those in need of care, I know that community health care centres and out patient services exist, but I don't really know much else about them. If I had to, I would know how to get help, but I've never actually put it into practice as yet. I went to an advice centre once and took part in a group discussion there. Frankly it was a bit disappointing. I wanted to be informed about special tricks which carers can use specifically in the case of Alzheimer's disease, tricks which I don't already know. There was nothing like that. All that happened was that everybody moaned about their own problems at home. That's not me at all, I don't like talking about my problems, and I don't have any either, I manage fine here. For example my wife's urinary incontinence is very limiting, it's a big handicap for her. It took a while until I worked out how to deal with it, the right pants, how to put them on and so on. But now everything is fine. It would have been nice to talk to someone at the beginning. I could have done with a bit of advice four or five years ago. But there wasn't anyone. I just tried out everything myself; that's also to do with my profession. After all, in my job I had to be - at least in the field of technology - extremely creative. It was me who always had to make the decisions, I had to find my own way, and you can see the same thing now in my housekeeping. These days everything is so easy, what with frozen food etc. Of course there are some situations which aren't so pleasant. The urinary incontinence is not so bad because of the special pants. I take her to the toilet now and again or I have to remind her. Changing the pants three times a day seems to work quite well. Sometimes she soils her pants and then I put her under the shower. Then it's a real mess. Our shower is in the cellar, but I mange OK. Once or twice a week I give my wife a shower, then I'm usually wetter than she is at the end !

I have a very good relationship with my eldest daughter who is very conscientious, we see her a lot. Sometimes I just put my wife in the car and we drive over to her place, we still manage that. My wife still recognises our daughter and her family and can still get about there. It's a familiar environment for her. As for our youngest daughter who lives in the house, we don't get on with her as well. It just doesn't work.

My main worry is that I stay healthy. I suffer from a bit of diabetes but it's not a big problem, I'm on top of it. Otherwise I'm as fit as a fiddle and I just hope I stay that way. If I wasn't able to do it, I really couldn't say what would happen. Until now I haven't had a break from looking after her, not a single day; I'm stuck here. Recently I was invited to a party at my old company, but then there was a problem of what to do with my wife. It would be nice if I wasn't so tied to the house, if I had a little more freedom. Nursing on an hourly basis could be a big help here. I think it would be good if the same person could come each time.

I never actively decided to take over the nursing of my wife, it just turned out that way. We have had a wonderful harmonious life together all these years, and it goes without saying that when one of us is sick, the other takes over. It happened so slowly, it just crept up on us. First she began to lose her memory. Now there is no speech at all, she can't speak any more. Now all she can do is express pleasure or displeasure by shaking her head or nodding, by gesticulating, that's all. She understands most things, although sometimes you have to repeat them. She can't write any more or use the phone and a lot of her old friends have died or drifted away. Nevertheless she doesn't suffer any great pain.

Gardening is my main hobby. Indoors I spend most of my time at do-it-yourself and although looking after my wife means that time is that bit shorter nowadays, I don't regret it in the slightest. Looking after my wife causes me no physical or mental strain. I used to do a lot of sport and all that hard training is paying off now. I've still got a bit left in me yet."

NOBODY WILL CARE FOR US AS WE CARE FOR THE OLD LADY

Dolores cares for her mother in law who is now eighty seven years and totally dependent, for even the most elementary things. She herself is fifty two years old and spends the day looking after the old lady. She can only manage the little business she has in the small rural town where they live in Southern Portugal, when the care of the old lady allows some spare time. Occasionally her husband helps her. The couple have no children and Dolores felt resigned to sacrificing herself to curing:

"During our youth they controlled us a lot. They always created obstacles when we wanted to go out, and since we didn't have any money and my husband's health wasn't very good we accepted their will. As a result we've never had a vacation. My mother used to tell me that one can't have everything in life, so if I had a loving husband I had to resign myself to other things. And I have resigned myself to this type of life, I've adapted to my mother-in law. I respect her wishes and try to avoid any problems. She has always been the owner of the house and still is. She's never raised her voice to me, she's always been a quiet woman, but she's hurt me a lot. I used to tell everything to my mother but when I came here I had to keep quiet. Nobody said anything to me, everything was very closed. Luckily my husband is very loving and a nice person.

I've always been very home loving and now when I go out in the street I feel as though I'm on another planet. I can't go anywhere, it's a problem when I have to go to the doctor in Lerida (the capital of the province). I haven't even been to see my own mother, who's very sick, for the past three years. I'd like to go and see her but I can't do it. I'm afraid of getting on and off the train. I'm very afraid of something happening to me and being alone.

For over a year now we've had to do everything for my mother-in-law, feed her, clean her dribbles, everything. She doesn't have any strength to do anything, but she's very aware of what's going on around her. She can't move at all. We have to get up at night, between three and four o'clock, to take her to the lavatory for her needs. My husband and I dress her, pick her up and do everything for her.

My husband has bad health, he's had bronchitis since he was young. He helps me but can't do much. Between the store and the house I don't stop the whole day. In the afternoons I sit down a bit to watch TV, its my only entertainment. I have stomach problems and go to the hospital in Lerida. I also have varicose veins which hurt a lot. What bothers me the most are my depressions and vertigo. My eyes hurt me and sometimes I fall down. I have lumbago pains in my legs and have to sit down often.

The house belongs to my mother-in-law. She's now eighty seven and has another son who lives nearby but with whom she doesn't get along very well. In these towns, in the poorer families, the heir stays at home. My husband and I have spent all the money we've had in fixing the house.

She's very afraid of being left alone. If we go out she doesn't accept anybody else staying with her. The last time we went out was four years ago to go to a wedding. On the way back our car broke down and we arrived home late. The person taking care of her was in such a state of nerves that she said she wouldn't do it again. Sundays we even go to different Masses so that one of us is always with her. We don't go out anywhere, we've made that quite clear. We don't go out because of her. It's normal, she needs somebody with her all the time. Besides if my husband can't go out, I don't go either, and if it's me who can't go out he won't go. I really like her, and she likes me too. To take care of her is not a sacrifice because I like doing it, it makes me feel good.

I have always seen the future very black, I'm very pessimistic. While I have my husband I have everything. If we make it to old age we will go to a nursing home. Nobody will care for us as we care for the old lady."

MY PROFESSION HAS ALWAYS BEEN CARING

Antonia is a sixty two year old woman taking care of her ninety year old father who depends on her for all everyday activities. She suffers from diabetes and arthritis and has had cancer and looking after her father represents a cost to her own health. For decades another sister had cared for her father but after a health crisis and hospitalization there was a confrontation with the previous carer and her family and the old man came to live with Antonia. The family, originally from the south, migrated to work in the industrial region of Barcelona; the old man had nine children. Antonia is married with two children.

"My profession has always been caring, for my husband and kids and now my father. The household consists of my husband, who works as a stoker in a ceramics factory, my twenty year old daughter Laura, who works in an office, the grandfather and myself. They brought him here to die two years ago. He was sent from the hospital to die here. We were told that he could last from six days to two months, and he still goes on. He says I have revived him! When they brought him from the hospital the doctor came to see him and she said he wouldn't last more than six days. Now he is better than I am, at least he runs around more than I do, his legs are quite agile. It may be because since he came here he's well taken care of.

My oldest brother asked me to do it. My other brother Antonio said to me "Look, the best thing is for him to stay with you, we cannot have him, and besides it will only be for a short time." I told him that I was sick and couldn't care for him as well, but I saw that the situation was very bad so I thought: Let him come, we'll manage. The decision to bring him here was not very difficult. When they discharged him from the hospital he had to go somewhere and he came with us because it is the law of life. If I didn't shelter him he would have had to go into a nursing home and since he is my father I took him in. All my siblings are very happy that he is here, they all know he is well taken care of. They come from time to time to visit him, mainly at holiday times.

We have to take care of everything. My husband washes his face with soap, and I wash the rest of him, his intimate parts and everything. I lie him down on the bed and wash him, because he can't get into the tub. I can't pick him up by myself to change his diaper, it hurts my back. My sister-in-law told me not to do it alone any more. One of my nieces sometimes helps me.

I have been sick myself, I had cancer and had to have therapy; since then I get tired easily. They operated on me recently. I went to the doctor because I had problems with my kidney, they did some tests and asked me to come into hospital. I was there for three months feeling very bad. My sister-in-law came everyday and took care of him and at night my husband took care of him. My aunt also came sometimes and helped. When I returned home my sister-in-law wouldn't let me do anything. She even cared for the grandfather, gave him breakfast and everything.

His worst problem is his mind, sometimes he see insects on the walls. Today when I arrived he said to me "Turn off the TV because they're going to break it, there's a bike climbing up the wall." He sees women walking around the house, and I say to him that it's the TV. When we turn it off then he says that everybody is gone. At night he doesn't want to go to bed before we do.

I had health problems before but since taking care of my father I've got worse and it's a heavy physical burden. It seems to get worse and worse. When I get very tired I sit down for a while and when I've recovered a bit I continue with the work. My daughter helps me most of the mornings. She gives him breakfast, and sometimes she washes his feet. My husband also helps. My father scolds me and tells me to sit down, not to work any more. If I don't eat he scolds me, he watches me having breakfast to make sure I eat everything. When I'm late he worries, he starts saying that maybe something has happened, he wonders where I am. He's very concerned about me.

You learn how to care, you get experience and when you love the person then even more so. It's difficult for other people to help you. If you have to care for a person of your own blood, you simply care for them, but I don't think I could do it for a stranger. But of course I do it for my father. To be honest, at the beginning it felt outrageous when I had to wash him, because he is my father. I felt embarrassed to wash him. My sister-in-law encouraged me, she was used to doing it.

I can't go to too many places because we can't leave him alone, so we are kind of slaves trapped here. When I go to the curandero (popular healer) my sister helps me, she comes to visit him. The only free time I have is when I go to the curandero. Before I had my father here I used to go out, see friends and neighbours, but since he's here I don't go out at all. Everybody knows me and talks to me, but I can't spend any time talking on the street or in the store.

When I see him not eating I get worried, and if I see him well then I'm happy. When I go to the bakery and see a nice biscuit or anything else nice I take it to him; he only has a few days of life left and has to enjoy them. When the doctor came and asked about his eating I answered that he ate anything he wanted. She told me I was doing the right thing."

HAVE I LET HIM DOWN, MADE THE WRONG DECISION?

Signe is a 72 year old woman looking after her husband Peder who is aged 85. In fact at the time of the interview, Peder had just moved into a nursing home, but when Signe was looking after him they had lived in a flat in a small provincial town in Jutland in Denmark on their own. Signe now lives there alone but has two children living not so far away.

"I was so unhappy when Peder moved into the nursing home. Of course, I can see that I'm getting old too and was having difficulty, but the children took the initiative to have him moved. They thought it was too much of a strain for me and I suppose it was too, but I didn't like the idea. I'd always promised him that he'd never go into a nursing home. I was worried sick when he went. Have I let him down, made the wrong decision? You know. It's not easy when you've been married for 50 years or so, seeing him go. But in a way, you know, it's as if it wasn't really him going into a home, not really Peder, no. He wouldn't want it, but thank goodness, he doesn't realize what's going on.

I'm happier now. Well no, not happier, resigned I suppose. You know, I've done my duty, you might say, looking after him at home for as long as I could. Some would have given up earlier I think. 15 years, it's a long time, isn't it? He was very dependent on me, and he was suffering severely from dementia. And that's a burden for both of us, though God only knows if he knew what it was like, I doubt it. I could get so mad sometimes, I felt all alone with the problem and knew very little about it all. The dementia developed very slowly, gradually. First there were things he needed help with, but I never really gave it much thought, you know, that I was now in a caring situation. He was my husband and I did what had to be done, that's all. And then it got worse, the dementia. In the end, I had to give up my office job, but we coped financially. Never had any problems like that.

We had help from the home help who would come and help me wash him, do the cooking, help getting him to the toilet and so on. Very good she was. He couldn't dress himself, but we managed that together. And sometimes he'd get so mad with her that he wouldn't let her wash him. What a battle we had with him sometimes, and he was as strong as an ox, you know. Funny looking back on it now.

It was a 24 hour a day job. He was always getting up in the night so I couldn't sleep properly for fear of him hurting himself or even wandering off. The district nurse would come, just to check him really, not to help, not unless he had to have medicines. But there was one year where he was just terrible at night so I had a night nurse from the council. She'd sit and keep an eye on him so I could sleep, but still you always have one eye and ear open. Even so, it was a help.

Yes, I think we received a lot of help from the Council. He had a special armchair and we got free nappies because he couldn't always get to the toilet. He hated that and so did I. I once applied for a temporary respite place for him, I felt that I'd go mad if I didn't get a break. But I didn't get one and I'm still here. You cope you know, you have to, don't you?

A typical day? That's difficult. There was a lot of routine, obviously, but no two days were really alike. The last 5 years he'd had a place at the local day centre and they picked him up in the mornings and brought him home in the bus. That gave me time to do all the jobs around the flat. No, I didn't see it as a rest, just as an opportunity to catch up as it were.

I always tried to get up first so I could wash and get breakfast. After breakfast I'd wash him and dress him if I could. Otherwise I'd wait for the home help to come. Then during the week he was picked up at about 9.30 and taken to the day centre and he came back just after lunch at about 2 o'clock. While he was away I'd do the cleaning, the shopping and the like. In the afternoon I'd try and occupy him and prepare supper at the same time. And then I'd put him to bed. Mind you, it didn't stop there. Like I say - 24 hours a day. You can't rest. Once he wandered off in the middle of the night and I had to have the police out to find him. Nothing happened, he came to no harm, and the two young policemen took it all very nicely, but it gave me a terrible shock. So after that I never let him out of my sight unless I knew someone was with him. And, you know, knowing what he was like used to worry me about what would happen if I was ill or whatever.

I've had no holiday for many years, I just couldn't face it. The last three years I wasn't even able to visit our children and missed that a lot, yes.

At my age there are not that many friends left to talk to about it all, but the children were always prepared to listen, even if I phoned them in the middle of the night. They've been lovely and even though I was upset that they insisted on him going into a nursing home, I know they did it for me. And that's alright now. Also I had been in a self-help group locally so I'd had them to share it all with. I still go along, even though he's away now and I don't have the same caring role.

I shall probably treat myself to a trip to Copenhagen soon. I haven't been there for years. Yes, I shall do that, it'll do me good."

NOW I'M ALL ON MY OWN LIKE A DRY TREE IN THE FOREST

Myrsini is an 82 year old widow living in a remote mountain cottage on the edge of a village in the Greek island of Lesbos. The previous day she had buried her brother, for whom she had cared for 10 years. Before that she had also cared for her mother, her husband and another brother and was expecting to have to care for the last brother at sometime in the future. While receiving a condolence visit from a niece and great nephew, who normally lived abroad, she talked about her life.

"Two years he was in bed. He couldn't even get out to the toilet. I cleaned him up in his room four times a week; everything had to be done inside, you see. It all ended on Saturday night. I looked after my mother too and I also had Eleni and Panayotis. I've been slaving away caring for over 18 years, all on my own without anyone even bringing a glass of water to help. Others get paid for doing this work, but I, who've cared for so many people for so many years, don't. Panayiotis was bedridden for two years, my mother for six years and this one here for ten years; he was OK for eight years but bedridden for the last two. He used to wander around the village - he'd lost his memory. All that torture. And my husband died in just a month. I was sitting in that chair there.

If I had a husband or children to help me it would be different but I've had to do all the caring alone. I took money, went to the priest - now I've got to go to the carpenter and pay for the coffin to finish with it all...

I've only got OGA pension (Agricultural Workers' pension) but some who've looked after sick people at home get other money from the welfare. Me, nothing. To go to the Welfare I'd have to get to Mytilene, but I'm tired of doing it all on my own. Two months ago they told me to go there to see about getting some money. A girl came here and gave me 15,000 drachmas (58 ECU) "That's all" she said. I said

"Why, I've worked for so many years and the welfare only gives me 15,000 drachmas?" "That's it" she says, "there's no more." But the others? They get something every month. Why? Eh? Why? They might just as well give me nothing. They gave me a cheque and the bank said I'd have to pay half the money for them to change it; I told them they might as well keep it all. Then I went to the Village Council and he said "You have to pay for them to change it for you." I've a cousin who's a driver so I went to his house and gave him it and he changed it in Mytilene and brought me the money. Otherwise they'd have kept a quarter of it.

I'm ill, I've got my heart, blood pressure, 19, 20, 19. I used to take one tablet for my blood pressure, now the doctors have made it three and one for my heart makes four, and one for the stomach at night, five! My liver is wrecked by now. This house is all I've got, neither husband, nor children, nor fields. Nothing, just the 10,000 drachmas (38.5 ECU a month) that I get.

My brother was 82 years old and a heavy old man. He was'nt a baby! Since January he was paralysed and couldn't get out of the house. He took to his bed. I had an old silte (a heavy leather waterproof undersheet) and I nursed him on the floor. I'd pull him to one side, change him, shake the clothes and covers, pull him back again and cover him up. I fed him every morning, midday and evening. He couldn't even hold a glass of water to drink for the past nine months. Previously I'd get his food ready and he'd eat it by himself. But the last months he was really bad. Only I know how I managed to care for him. I washed everything by hand. I'd warm up the water, put in soap powder, dirty clothes, I didn't even put my hands in just beat them with a stick. The tap's inside, I'd put the hose on the tap to rinse them. What else could I do? No one comes to help you with these things. No! Who would come. No one bothers about you. If I only had a sister, children (sons), a daughter. Where are they?

If I didn't have this room where would I've put him? In this room I've nursed my brother, mother and now this one. Every year and a half I buried someone. Mr. Statis said to me one day "You're a real heroine. Go and lie down for a bit." The others have all died and there's just one left for me as a dowry! I've had them all. I should rest in peace once and for all, if only it would happen as I'm sitting here I'd escape any more torture. I can't even talk about it all any more, or think about it. I just can't.

I'm 77 now and I've looked after the three of them but who's going to look after me? Nobody. Not even a neighbour comes in here, there's nobody, nobody at all. I used to send a young girl for bread twice a week in the winter and I'd give her a few drachmas each time. But she stopped coming because it was'nt enough. I went down the other day for bread and saw a little watermelon, just two kilos, but how could I carry it? They don't come past the house any more or I don't hear them; I've lost my hearing. Anyway I found a lad and gave him 50 drachmas and he carried the watermelon and two loaves of bread home for me and I followed up the hill behind him - I had to stop four times to catch my breath. The doctor has told me "If you walk and get tired, sit down and rest." I can get to the village slowly.

I'd be ashamed to send anyone to an institution. No, no I'd never send them. I couldn't bear the guilt of that. The village president and the priests told me "You'll kill yourself looking after them all! What's going to happen?" I said "As long as I'm alive I'll look after them as well as I can. When I'm dead and can't see what's happening, do what you like." For goodness sake, send my mother or my father to an institution! Didn't they tire themselves out for us? Eh? So? As a family we got on all right, we never had any fields to fight over!

Sometimes I used to get angry with him. Once when I was trying to change him he'd not stand up, then he grabbed my arm so hard he left bruises. What can you do? Hit him? No. But he was really contrary; for the last week he'd not drink any water at all. If I took him a glass of water he wanted to drink from mine; if I took it from the fridge he wanted it from the tap. I'd bring the stool to sit and feed him and he'd not eat. He'd just push it aside and the food would go off and I'd have to throw it away. I'd say "What can I do with you? There's the cheese and olives." He'd just eat a little bread sometimes, just plain bread. He was really contrary, may God forgive him.

He was married once but divorced - it only lasted six months. She was as difficult as he was! And my other brother was'nt married either, two unmarried brothers in the village and I said to myself if only one of them had given me a sister in law, a couple of nieces. I've just three or four nephews and nieces and a brother in Athens who comes here for his summer holiday once a year. But not even a letter in the winter to ask how I'm on my own. Nobody comes. I sit here all alone every day and in the summer where can you go anyway? Even if I go to sit with the neighbours I'm so deaf that they chatter away and I can't hear what they're saying so I think they're gossiping about me. So I get up and leave. Just because I can't hear, do they need to make fun of me? deaf aids are expensive, I just can't manage to buy one. I don't have a TV or telephone. Not even a TV so I could see something when I sit all alone like an animal in a cage. I've a radio, but can I hear it? A TV does wake your brain up a bit. I don't even put the radio on now since I'm in mourning for forty days. We mourn properly here until the forty days are over.

I can't even go to the KAPI (Community Open Care Old People's Centre) in this heat. I go with the KAPI bus to the Health Centre every month for my prescription and then I go downstairs and drink a coffee or have an orangeade before going home. I've only got this one dress and it's old and too heavy and full of darns. Even if they see me like this, I couldn't care less. But who sees me anyway? I can't put my really thick dress on and I can't afford a new dress, it would be 3000 drachmas (12 ECU) and where can I find that, what can I buy with the 10,000 drachmas I get? I don't have any fields to rent out; just this house. Can I eat from the house?

The doctor has never been here. Once I asked him to visit and come and see my brother, but he said "Bring him to the Health Centre." How? He couldn't get up. Who was going to take him there? Another time he went to visit Mrs. Pezmazoglou and Stavros Michaelidis at home. So I complained to him; I said "Why did you go and see those two and you didn't come and see my brother?" He said "You didn't tell us to come." "Eh, I shouldn't have to tell you to come; you know I've had him two years in bed. Should I've to tell you to come?" How could I get him to the Health Centre? He couldn't get out of bed, his leg was rotting away, he was just skin and bones, he had no belly at all. Just a skeleton.

I don't pay anything for my drugs. Last month I went and said "It's my stomach." They gave me some hormones and I went and had some X-rays, there was a radiologist there and he gave me some other drugs, because the ones I was having were cheap rubbish. I've to take suppositories of course because the other drugs upset my stomach. I've drunk bottles of that white stuff but I've never seen any improvement, either from that or all the rest. If I don't take the suppository I don't sleep. If I take it at least I sleep from two to seven once or twice a week. The pharmacy used to be near here where the shops are, but when they built the new Health Centre it moved over there.

But I'm worse now and I've lost my courage. Consider what it's like when you have a man to care for and make sure he doesn't get bed sores, to change four times a week, all alone. Even changing a small child can be trouble. He smelled as well, How did I manage it?

Now I've to arrange the memorial service and prepare the koliva (funeral food for mourners of boiled wheat mixed with sugar and cinnamon, decorated with nuts and raisins). I've always paid the priest for the memorial services for my mother and brother and the rest. But when I die who'll make a plate of koliva for me, who'll light a candle for me, who'll make an offering of bread for my soul?

Now I'm all on my own like a dry tree in the forest. The wolves should come down and eat me one night to finish it all off!"

COMMENTARY

Each interview in this book presents a unique picture of people's lives as carers of older dependent people. Despite their many differences carers throughout the nine countries share common experiences that are the result of them bearing the burden of responsibility for caring for an adult who can no longer be independent. The physical toil and emotional stress associated with care, often generating health problems for carers themselves, are widely reported. However, so too is the emotional satisfaction that many carers derive from caring for a member of their own family whom they love and also the reciprocation of love and care given to them when they were younger.

In most cases there is usually a main family carer who undertakes most of the physical care and emotional support of the older, dependent person. In some extreme situations carers appear to be completely isolated, without friends, family or services to help them. In other cases carers receive important support from other family members, close friends and neighbours. In countries where services exist and are organised to support carers as well as older dependent people, the responsibility for physical care may be considerably relieved for carers as well as some of the psychological burden.

While anyone may become a carer there are evidently quite different probabilities depending on the kinship relationship to the elderly person, the availability of alternative caring solutions - whether these be other kin or services, and the personal relationship between the carer and the older person needing care. Caring situations vary greatly; some carers appear to have been involved for almost their whole lifetime in caring for other people, while for some carers it is an entirely new experience. Some receive support from their family, others care completely on their own or find caring conflicts with other family obligations. Husbands and wives in most countries want to care for their partner for as long as they're physically able, whatever this means in terms of sacrificing their own health and personal needs and wishes. The need to attend to the intimate personal care of their spouse may represent a problem initially but this is more easily accommodated within the framework of their personal intimacy and affection in a life spent together. Children and siblings who care are also affected strongly by the sense of duty to the other needing care, by the wish to repay in kind previous love and care, but at the same time they may be more aware of the sacrifices in their own lives. The intimate personal care of an older dependent person by a "child" and more particularly someone of the opposite sex, may represent a problem unless the carer learns to develop a detached "professional" attitude to the task involved.

Inevitably the experience of caring depends on the previous relationship between family members; some carers find caring cathartic and a new positive experience in their relationship with the dependent, elderly person, or with others in their family; an occasion to bind family members more closely together. Other carers find caring extremely stressful and destructive of their own lives. Some are able to use the experience of caring as a way of confronting problems in their previous relationship. For many carers the main experience is that of finding themselves absorbed by the hard physical grind of continuous, intensive care. The frustrations, stresses, anxieties and difficulties of care, especially when this is done without adequate support from others, give indications of what can lead to elder abuse and mistreatment. In some cases caring involves a self destructive form of altruism. Some women carers appear particularly prone to obliterating and suppressing their own personal needs, reflecting their experiences in society. Paid employment for all carers represents both an added stress - in that caring duties have to be combined with professional responsibilities - but also a way of keeping a separate identity and interests. Those carers with professional occupational experience are often those most able to cope subsequently with the many demands of caring, with finding services and support, and with maintaining a sense of their own needs.

Inevitably caring brings to the fore a whole gamut of emotions that relate to the carers having to confront the fact that a very significant person in their lives, a spouse, a sibling or a parent, is approaching the end of their own life. Carers have to face the fact of their own ageing and death and mourn for the elderly person who is no longer independent and whose original personality may be obliterated by illness.

Some people spend a lifetime caring whether this is for one older person or for a variety of dependents and although the intensity of caring varies over time nonetheless they will have spent a considerable part of their lives providing support for others. Some caring situations involve an intense but much shorter period of care, as for example in the case of acute illness. In countries where a variety of adequate residential facilities exist for older people needing long term care because of chronic illness, individual carers may have real choices about whether to care and for what length of time. In Member States which lack choices with respect to adequate residential care, many family carers have to accept that caring will continue for as long as the elderly person is alive. Unfortunately it is exactly in these same countries that other support facilities such as good primary health care, home care services and respite care for older people and their carers are least developed. Thus the full physical, emotional and financial burden of care falls most heavily on those who often have the least resources.

The main carer at any one point of time can vary and the designation may also reflect a carer's individual perspective. Thus for an elderly couple one spouse may be the main carer, but the child who supervises them and takes on major responsibility for their household and medical care may also see him/herself as the main carer. The situation provoking the need for care also changes over time; thus typically what an elderly carer may manage at one period of time may prove impossible at a more acute or later stage of physical and mental dependency leading to the need for new caring solutions.

Few older people, even with the onset of dependency, wish to give up their own home and live either in an institution or with their children. Carers too, unless already living with the older dependent person, may be unwilling to change their residential arrangements.

However, in the absence of adequate financial resources and support services for older people in their own homes, children may have to take on the responsibility of care, willingly or unwillingly, and this may have to include cohabitation under less than ideal circumstances.

Clearly carers' income and education play a significant role in their access to services and support and even as to how they approach the task of caring. In countries where Carers' Associations have developed, carers have a valuable additional resource providing both a stronger, united "political" voice and also psychological support and solidarity. In countries where neither the welfare state nor welfare citizenship are well developed individual carers have to depend almost entirely on their own personal and family resources to deal with their problems.

The carers who were interviewed were selected to show as wide a spectrum as possible of caring situations; however from this number no conclusions should be drawn as to the consequences of class, gender, ethnicity and culture on the experiences and needs of different groups of carers. Rural-urban differences do emerge in that in many rural regions of the Member States there are fewer services available to carers. Despite differences within and between countries, in income, education, occupation and residence, most carers share the common feeling of periodically being bowed down and exhausted by caring.

There are striking differences in the interviews in the availability of and access to services to support family carers and older, dependent people between countries and areas within countries. Where support services are well developed they help carers but do not relieve them of their responsibility for care which most would be unwilling to relinquish. Support services which encourage and teach family carers are evidently particularly valuable to them, since they can learn new skills and attitudes which may enable them to be more effective and to preserve their own needs and identities. The development of support services for carers by the public sector is also a way of publicly acknowledging and giving value to their work and contribution to individual and society's well being.

Increasing numbers of carers will have to contemplate looking after more than one elderly relative during their life time both because of the devreasing size of families and the greater longevity of older people. Some of these cases are illustrated in the interviews with carers; in the most extreme cases carers can spend a major part of their lives looking after various dependent, elderly relatives. As more stress is given to the preference for home care rather than residential care for elderly people, policy makers and service providers will have to publicly acknowledge the increasingly significant "army" of family carers and their needs for support. Social recognition through practical measures of support - whether these be in the form of services or financial resources - will be an increasingly significant way of supporting the elderly in the community and avoiding their marginalization as well as that of their family carers.

European Foundation for the Improvement of Living and Working Conditions

Carers Talking: Interviews with Family Cares of Older, Dependent People in the European Community

Luxembourg: Office for Official Publications of the European Communities

1993 – 118 p. – 16 x 23.4 cm

ISBN 92-826-6570-4

Price (excluding VAT) in Luxembourg: ECU 13.50

Venta y suscripciones • Salg og abonnement • Verkauf und Abonnement • Πωλήσεις και συνδρομές
Sales and subscriptions • Vente et abonnements • Vendita e abbonamenti
Verkoop en abonnementen • Venda e assinaturas

BELGIQUE / BELGIË

Moniteur belge /
Belgisch Staatsblad
Rue de Louvain 42 / Leuvenseweg 42
B-1000 Bruxelles / B-1000 Brussel
Tél. (02) 512 00 26
Fax (02) 511 01 84

Autres distributeurs /
Overige verkooppunten

Librairie européenne /
Europese boekhandel
Rue de la Loi 244 / Wetstraat 244
B-1040 Bruxelles / B-1040 Brussel
Tél. (02) 231 04 35
Fax (02) 735 08 60

Jean de Lannoy
Avenue du Roi 202 / Koningslaan 202
B-1060 Bruxelles / B-1060 Brussel
Tél. (02) 538 51 69
Télex 63220 UNBOOK B
Fax (02) 538 08 41

Document delivery:

Credoc
Rue de la Montagne 34 / Bergstraat 34
Bte 11 / Bus 11
B-1000 Bruxelles / B-1000 Brussel
Tél. (02) 511 69 41
Fax (02) 513 31 95

DANMARK

J. H. Schultz Information A/S
Herstedvang 10-12
DK-2620 Albertslund
Tlf. 43 63 23 00
Fax (Sales) 43 63 19 69
Fax (Management) 43 63 19 49

DEUTSCHLAND

Bundesanzeiger Verlag
Breite Straße 78-80
Postfach 10 05 34
D-50445 Köln
Tel. (02 21) 20 29-0
Telex ANZEIGER BONN 8 882 595
Fax 2 02 92 78

GREECE/ΕΛΛΑΔΑ

G.C. Eleftheroudakis SA
International Bookstore
Nikis Street 4
GR-10563 Athens
Tel. (01) 322 63 23
Telex 219410 ELEF
Fax 323 98 21

ESPAÑA

Boletín Oficial del Estado
Trafalgar, 29
E-28071 Madrid
Tel. (91) 538 22 95
Fax (91) 538 23 49

Mundi-Prensa Libros, SA
Castelló, 37
E-28001 Madrid
Tel. (91) 431 33 99 (Libros)
       431 32 22 (Suscripciones)
       435 36 37 (Dirección)
Télex 49370-MPLI-E
Fax (91) 575 39 98

Sucursal:

Librería Internacional AEDOS
Consejo de Ciento, 391
E-08009 Barcelona
Tel. (93) 488 34 92
Fax (93) 487 76 59

Llibreria de la Generalitat
de Catalunya
Rambla dels Estudis, 118 (Palau Moja)
E-08002 Barcelona
Tel. (93) 302 68 35
       302 64 62
Fax (93) 302 12 99

FRANCE

Journal officiel
Service des publications
des Communautés européennes
26, rue Desaix
F-75727 Paris Cedex 15
Tél. (1) 40 58 75 00
Fax (1) 40 58 77 00

IRELAND

Government Supplies Agency
4-5 Harcourt Road
Dublin 2
Tel. (1) 66 13 111
Fax (1) 47 80 645

ITALIA

Licosa SpA
Via Duca di Calabria, 1/1
Casella postale 552
I-50125 Firenze
Tel. (055) 64 54 15
Fax 64 12 57
Telex 570466 LICOSA I

GRAND-DUCHÉ DE LUXEMBOURG

Messageries du livre
5, rue Raiffeisen
L-2411 Luxembourg
Tél. 40 10 20
Fax 40 10 24 01

NEDERLAND

SDU Overheidsinformatie
Externe Fondsen
Postbus 20014
2500 EA's-Gravenhage
Tel. (070) 37 89 911
Fax (070) 34 75 778

PORTUGAL

Imprensa Nacional
Casa da Moeda, EP
Rua D. Francisco Manuel de Melo, 5
P-1092 Lisboa Codex
Tel. (01) 69 34 14

Distribuidora de Livros
Bertrand, Ld.ª
Grupo Bertrand, SA
Rua das Terras dos Vales, 4-A
Apartado 37
P-2700 Amadora Codex
Tel. (01) 49 59 050
Telex 15798 BERDIS
Fax 49 60 255

UNITED KINGDOM

HMSO Books (Agency section)
HMSO Publications Centre
51 Nine Elms Lane
London SW8 5DR
Tel. (071) 873 9090
Fax 873 8463
Telex 29 71 138

ÖSTERREICH

Manz'sche Verlags-
und Universitätsbuchhandlung
Kohlmarkt 16
A-1014 Wien
Tel. (0222) 531 61-133
Telex 112 500 BOX A
Fax (0222) 531 61-181

SUOMI/FINLAND

Akateeminen Kirjakauppa
Keskuskatu 1
PO Box 128
SF-00101 Helsinki
Tel. (0) 121 41
Fax (0) 121 44 41

NORGE

Narvesen Info Center
Bertrand Narvesens vei 2
PO Box 6125 Etterstad
N-0602 Oslo 6
Tel. (22) 57 33 00
Telex 79668 NIC N
Fax (22) 68 19 01

SVERIGE

BTJ AB
Traktorvägen 13
S-22100 Lund
Tel. (046) 18 00 00
Fax (046) 18 01 25
         30 79 47

SCHWEIZ / SUISSE / SVIZZERA

OSEC
Stampfenbachstraße 85
CH-8035 Zürich
Tel. (01) 365 54 49
Fax (01) 365 54 11

ČESKÁ REPUBLIKA

NIS ČR
Havelkova 22
130 00 Praha 3
Tel. (2) 235 84 46
Fax (2) 235 97 88

MAGYARORSZÁG

Euro-Info-Service
Club Sziget
Margitsziget
1138 Budapest
Tel./Fax 1 111 60 61
         1 111 62 16

POLSKA

Business Foundation
ul. Krucza 38/42
00-512 Warszawa
Tel. (22) 21 99 93, 628-28 82
International Fax & Phone
         (0-39) 12-00-77

ROMÂNIA

Euromedia
65, Strada Dionisie Lupu
70184 Bucuresti
Tel./Fax 0 12 96 46

BĂLGARIJA

Europress Klassica BK Ltd
66, bd Vitosha
1463 Sofia
Tel./Fax 2 52 74 75

RUSSIA

CCEC
9,60-letiya Oktyabrya Avenue
117312 Moscow
Tel./Fax (095) 135 52 27

CYPRUS

Cyprus Chamber of Commerce and
Industry
Chamber Building
38 Grivas Dhigenis Ave
3 Deligiorgis Street
PO Box 1455
Nicosia
Tel. (2) 449500/462312
Fax (2) 458630

MALTA

Miller distributors Ltd
Scots House, M.A. Vassalli street
PO Box 272
Valletta
Tel. 24 73 01
Fax 23 49 14

TÜRKIYE

Pres Gazete Kitap Dergi
Pazarlama Dağitim Ticaret ve sanayi
AŞ
Narlibahçe Sokak N. 15
Istanbul-Cağaloğlu
Tel. (1) 520 92 96 - 528 55 66
Fax 520 64 57
Telex 23822 DSVO-TR

ISRAEL

ROY International
PO Box 13056
41 Mishmar Hayarden Street
Tel. Aviv 61130
Tel. 3 496 108
Fax 3 544 60 39

UNITED STATES OF AMERICA/
CANADA

UNIPUB
4611-F Assembly Drive
Lanham, MD 20706-4391
Tel. Toll Free (800) 274 4888
Fax (301) 459 0056

CANADA

Subscriptions only
Uniquement abonnements

Renouf Publishing Co. Ltd
1294 Algoma Road
Ottawa, Ontario K1B 3W8
Tel. (613) 741 43 33
Fax (613) 741 54 39
Telex 0534783

AUSTRALIA

Hunter Publications
58A Gipps Street
Collingwood
Victoria 3066
Tel. (3) 417 5361
Fax (3) 419 7154

JAPAN

Kinokuniya Company Ltd
17-7 Shinjuku 3- Chome
Shinjuku-ku
Tokyo 160-91
Tel. (03) 3439-0121

Journal Department
PO Box 55 Chitose
Tokyo 156
Tel. (03) 3439-0124

SOUTH-EAST ASIA

Legal Library Services Ltd
STK Agency
Robinson Road
PO Box 1817
Singapore 9036

SOUTH AFRICA

Safto
5th Floor, Export House
Cnr Maude & West Streets
Sandton 2146
Tel. (011) 883-3737
Fax (011) 883-6569

AUTRE PAYS
OTHER COUNTRIES
ANDERE LÄNDER

Office des publications officielles
des Communautés européennes
2, rue Mercier
L-2985 Luxembourg
Tél. 499 28 -1
Télex PUBOF LU 1324 b
Fax 48 85 73/48 68 17

7/93

**Bibliothèques
Université d'Ottawa
Echéance**

**Libraries
University of Ottawa
Date Due**